CELEBRATION OF ST

West

Peter Waller

IAN ALLAN Publishing

Acknowledgements

I am very conscious that this book would not have been possible without the effort of many photographers. In particular I would like to thank: Roy Brook; Kenneth Field (whose book *Pennine Steam* was — and is — an excellent portrait of steam in the area); Geoff Lumb; Brian Morrison; and Gavin Morrison. All timetables illustrated come from the author's collection.

First published 1994

ISBN 0 7110 2252 6

Published by Ian Allan Publishing

an imprint of Ian Allan Ltd, Terminal House, Station Approach, Shepperton, Surrey TW17 8AS.
Printed by Ian Allan Printing Ltd, Coombelands House, Addlestone, Weybridge, Surrey KT15 1HY.

Cover photos supplied by Gavin Morrison

Title page:
'V2' No 60886 battles up the 1 in 70 gradient between Bardsey and Thorner with the 11-coach Saturdays Only Newcastle-Llandudno service on 19 August 1961. By 1961, this was the only long-distance scheduled steam-hauled service to operate over the line via Wetherby. *M. Mitchell*

This page:
Patricroft-allocated BR Standard Class 5 No 73045 creates plenty of smoke near Golcar on the climb out of Huddersfield on the ex-LNWR main line with the Saturdays Only 10.48am Filey Holiday Camp-Manchester service on 5 August 1967. This may well have been amongst the last workings for this particular locomotive as it was withdrawn during this particular month and consigned for scrap to Cashmores at Newport. *M. Mitchell*

Contents

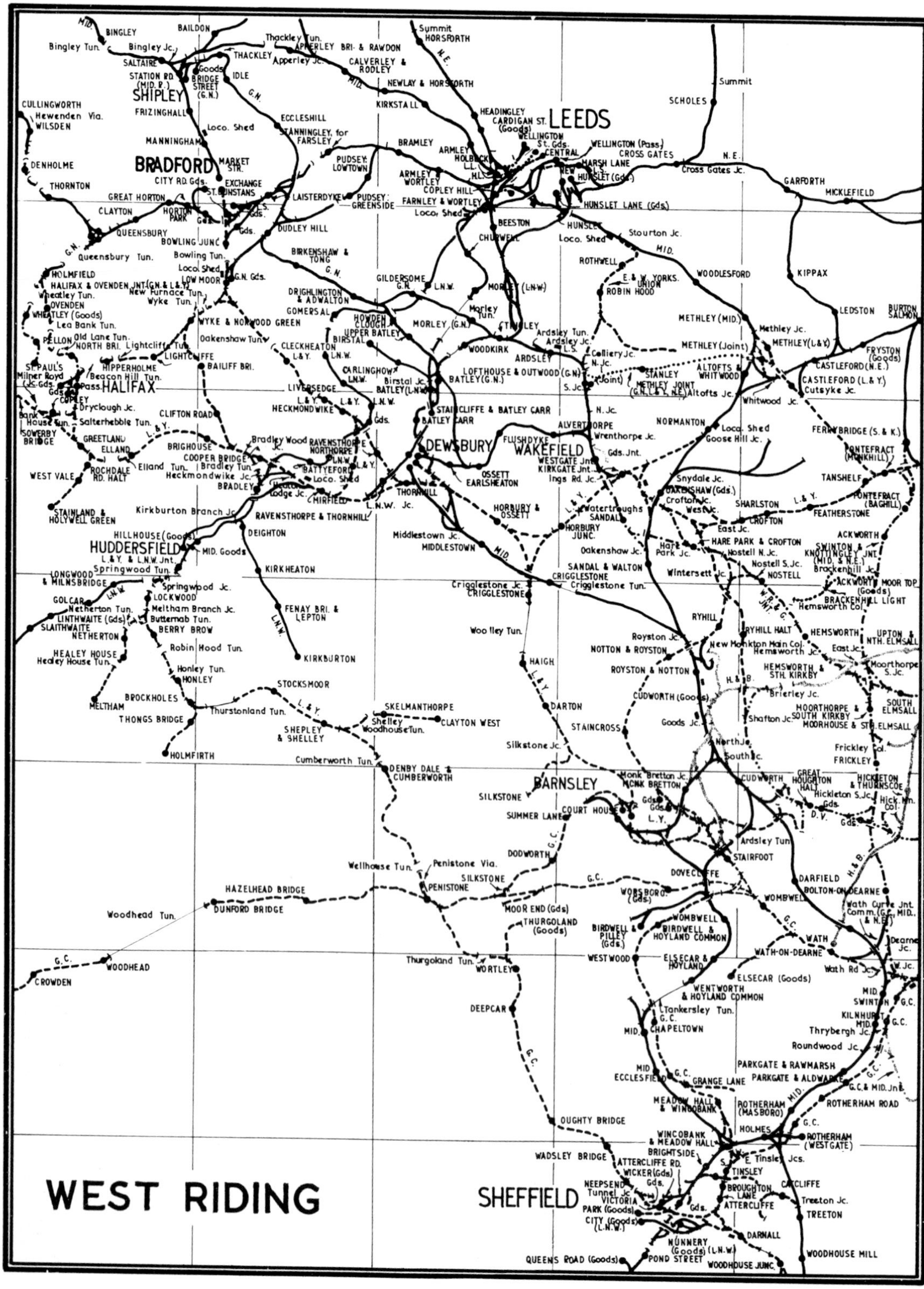
WEST RIDING
LEEDS
BRADFORD
SHIPLEY
HALIFAX
HUDDERSFIELD
DEWSBURY
WAKEFIELD
BARNSLEY
SHEFFIELD
BINGLEY
Bingley Tun.
Bingley Jc.
BAILDON
SALTAIRE
STATION RD. (MID. R.)
BRIDGE STREET (G.N.)
Goods
THACKLEY
Thackley Tun.
APPERLEY BRI. & RAWDON
Apperley Jc.
IDLE
CALVERLEY & RODLEY
NEWLAY & HORSFORTH
Summit
HORSFORTH
KIRKSTALL
HEADINGLEY
CARDIGAN ST. (Goods)
WELLINGTON St. Gds.
CENTRAL
WELLINGTON (Pass.)
MARSH LANE
CROSS GATES
Cross Gates Jc.
SCHOLES
GARFORTH
MICKLEFIELD
CULLINGWORTH
Hewenden Via.
WILSDEN
DENHOLME
THORNTON
FRIZINGHALL
MANNINGHAM
Loco. Shed
MARKET STR.
EXCHANGE
CITY RD. Gds.
ST. DUNSTANS
ECCLESHILL
STANNINGLEY, for FARSLEY
PUDSEY LOWTOWN
PUDSEY GREENSIDE
LAISTERDYKE
BRAMLEY
ARMLEY
ARMLEY & WORTLEY
COPLEY HILL
FARNLEY & WORTLEY
Loco. Shed
HOLBECK
HUNSLET (Gds.)
HUNSLET LANE (Gds.)
HUNSLET
Loco. Shed
Stourton Jc.
BEESTON
CHURWELL
GREAT HORTON
CLAYTON
HORTON PARK
QUEENSBURY
Queensbury Tun.
BOWLING JUNC.
Bowling Tun.
DUDLEY HILL
BIRKENSHAW & TONG
GILDERSOME
MORLEY (L.N.W.)
ROTHWELL
E. & W. YORKS. UNION
ROBIN HOOD
WOODLESFORD
KIPPAX
HOLMFIELD
HALIFAX & OVENDEN JNT. (G.N. & L.&Y.)
Wheatley Tun.
OVENDEN
WHEATLEY (Goods)
Lea Bank Tun.
PELLON
Old Lane Tun.
NORTH BRI.
Lightcliffe Tun.
LIGHTCLIFFE
HIPPERHOLME
Beacon Hill Tun.
ST. PAUL'S
Milner Royd Jc.
Pass.
COPLEY
Dryclough Jc.
Salterhebble Tun.
SOWERBY BRIDGE
GREETLAND
ELLAND
Elland Tun.
WEST VALE
ROCHDALE RD. HALT
STAINLAND & HOLYWELL GREEN
LOW MOOR
New Furnace Tun.
Wyke Tun.
WYKE & NORWOOD GREEN
Oakenshaw Tun.
BAILIFF BRI.
CLIFTON ROAD
BRIGHOUSE
COOPER BRIDGE
Bradley Tun.
Heckmondwike Jc.
BRADLEY
DRIGHLINGTON & ADWALTON
GOMERSAL
CLECKHEATON
LIVERSEDGE
HECKMONDWIKE
HOWDEN CLOUGH
UPPER BATLEY
BIRSTAL
CARLINGHOW
Birstal Jc.
BATLEY (L.N.W.)
MORLEY (G.N.)
Morley Tun.
TINGLEY
WOODKIRK
ARDSLEY
Ardsley Tun.
Ardsley Jc.
LOFTHOUSE & OUTWOOD (G.N.)
BATLEY (G.N.)
Colliery Jc.
STANLEY
METHLEY JOINT
Altofts Jc.
METHLEY (MID.)
METHLEY (Joint)
Methley Jc.
METHLEY (L&Y)
ALTOFTS & WHITWOOD
LEDSTON
BURTON SALMON
FRYSTON (Goods)
CASTLEFORD (N.E.)
CASTLEFORD (L.& Y.)
Cutsyke Jc.
Whitwood Jc.
STAINCLIFFE & BATLEY CARR
NORMANTON
ALVERTHORPE
Wrenthorpe Jc.
Loco. Shed
Goose Hill Jc.
FERRYBRIDGE (S. & K.)
PONTEFRACT (MONKHILL)
Bradley Wood Jc.
RAVENSTHORPE
NORTHORPE
BATTYEFORD
Loco. Shed
MIRFIELD
FLUSHDYKE
WESTGATE
KIRKGATE Jnt.
Ings Rd. Jc.
Gds. Jnt.
OSSETT
EARLSHEATON
THORNHILL
Snydale Jc.
OAKENSHAW (Gds.)
Crofton Jc.
TANSHELF
PONTEFRACT (BAGHILL)
FEATHERSTONE
Kirkburton Branch Jc.
RAVENSTHORPE & THORNHILL
L.N.W. Jc.
HORBURY & OSSETT
Watertroughs
SANDAL
SHARLSTON
CROFTON
East Jc.
HILLHOUSE (Goods)
Loco. Shed
DEIGHTON
HORBURY JUNC.
HARE PARK & CROFTON
ACKWORTH
MID. Goods
L.&Y. & L.N.W. Jnt.
Springwood Tun.
Middlestown Jc.
MIDDLESTOWN
Oakenshaw Jc.
Hare Park Jc.
Nostell N. Jc.
Nostell S. Jc.
SWINTON & KNOTTINGLEY JNT. (MID. & N.E.)
Brackenhill Jc.
LONGWOOD & MILNSBRIDGE
Springwood Jc.
LOCKWOOD
KIRKHEATON
SANDAL & WALTON
CRIGGLESTONE
Wintersett Jc.
NOSTELL
ACKWORTH MOOR TOP (Goods)
GOLCAR
Netherton Tun.
LINTHWAITE (Gds.)
SLAITHWAITE
NETHERTON
Meltham Branch Jc.
Butternab Tun.
BERRY BROW
FENAY BRI. & LEPTON
Crigglestone Jc.
CRIGGLESTONE
Crigglestone Tun.
BRACKENHILL LIGHT
Hemsworth Col.
RYHILL
RYHILL HALT
HEMSWORTH
UPTON & NTH. ELMSALL
Royston Jc.
New Monkton Main Col.
Hemsworth Jc.
East Jc.
Moorthorpe S. Jc.
HEALEY HOUSE
Healey House Tun.
Robin Hood Tun.
Honley Tun.
HONLEY
KIRKBURTON
Woolley Tun.
HAIGH
NOTTON & ROYSTON
ROYSTON & NOTTON
HEMSWORTH & STH. KIRKBY
STOCKSMOOR
BROCKHOLES
MELTHAM
THONGS BRIDGE
Thurstonland Tun.
SKELMANTHORPE
Shelley Woodhouse Tun.
CLAYTON WEST
SHEPLEY & SHELLEY
DARTON
STAINCROSS
CUDWORTH (Goods)
Brierley Jc.
Goods
Shafton Jc.
MOORTHORPE & SOUTH KIRKBY
MOORHOUSE & STH. ELMSALL
SOUTH ELMSALL
HOLMFIRTH
Cumberworth Tun.
DENBY DALE & CUMBERWORTH
Silkstone Jc.
North Jc.
South Jc.
Frickley Col.
FRICKLEY
SILKSTONE
Monk Bretton Jc.
MONK BRETTON
CUDWORTH
GREAT HOUGHTON HALT
HICKLETON & THURNSCOE
Hickleton S. Jc.
SUMMER LANE
COURT HOUSE
Ardsley Tun.
STAIRFOOT
DODWORTH
Wellhouse Tun.
Penistone Via.
PENISTONE
SILKSTONE
DOVECLIFFE
WORSBORO' (Gds.)
WOMBWELL
DARFIELD
BOLTON-ON-DEARNE
HAZELHEAD BRIDGE
DUNFORD BRIDGE
Woodhead Tun.
MOOR END (Gds.)
THURGOLAND (Goods)
BIRDWELL & PILLEY (Gds.)
BIRDWELL & HOYLAND COMMON
Wath Curve Jnt. Comm. (G.C., MID., & N.E.)
WATH
WATH-ON-DEARNE
Dearne Jc.
CROWDEN
WOODHEAD
Thurgoland Tun.
WORTLEY
WESTWOOD
ELSECAR & HOYLAND
ELSECAR (Goods)
Wath Rd. Jc.
W. Jc.
DEEPCAR
WENTWORTH & HOYLAND COMMON
Tankersley Tun.
CHAPELTOWN
SWINTON
KILNHURST
Thrybergh Jc.
Roundwood Jc.
ECCLESFIELD
GRANGE LANE
PARKGATE & RAWMARSH
PARKGATE & ALDWARKE
G.C. & MID. Jnt.
MEADOW HALL & WINCOBANK
ROTHERHAM (MASBORO')
ROTHERHAM ROAD
OUGHTY BRIDGE
WINCOBANK & MEADOW HALL
HOLMES
ROTHERHAM (WESTGATE)
BRIGHTSIDE
WADSLEY BRIDGE
ATTERCLIFFE RD.
WICKER (Gds.)
E. Tinsley Jcs.
TINSLEY
NEEPSEND
Tunnel Jc.
VICTORIA
PARK (Goods)
CITY (Goods) (L.N.W.)
BROUGHTON LANE
ATTERCLIFFE
CATCLIFFE
Treeton Jc.
TREETON
DARNALL
NUNNERY (Goods) (L.N.W.)
QUEENS ROAD (Goods)
POND STREET
WOODHOUSE JUNC.
WOODHOUSE MILL
MID.
G.N.
N.E.
L.N.W.
L.&Y.
G.C.
H.&B.
W.R.&G.
D.V.

Introduction

The West Riding of Yorkshire is a county of contrasts; in the north it can lay claim to some of the most inhospitable landscape that England can offer, whilst in the east it incorporates much of the flat Vale of York; it possesses not one, but two centres of traditional industry — the textile district around Leeds and Bradford as well as the iron and steel industry of Sheffield and Rotherham — whilst also including rich agricultural land. It stretches from the estuary of the Humber, where the docks of Goole were in the county, almost across to the Irish Sea bisecting the country and providing within its broad acres almost a microcosm of the whole of England. And it had the additional advantage of being located above one of the richest coalfields in the country.

These various strands of environmental and economic circumstance were to play a crucial role in the railway development of the region. The early mineral lines, which abounded throughout the area, were designed to capture the industrial production of the region. From there it was but a short step towards the construction of lines for both passenger and freight services, and over a period of more than 70 years a massive and intricate network appeared. Many of the lines were built in direct competition and many must never have realised a profit for their promoters, but were seen as moves in a massive game of chess as railway companies sought to expand their areas of influence.

Although there were casualties before the railways were Nationalised in 1948, these were relatively few. But the onset of BR and its declining finances meant that closures became increasingly common. Modernisation came early to West Riding lines, as the first generation of diesel multiple-units arrived at Bradford Hammerton Street, but even these popular trains could do little to stem the losses. The West Riding, battleground for numerous of the pre-Grouping companies and later fought over by both the LMS and LNER, was to fall, initially, into three of the BR regions — the London Midland, North Eastern and Eastern. Inevitably, as the years passed, the regional boundaries were to be modified, with sheds and lines passing from one region to another. Eventually, concurrent with the demise of steam in the area, the NER was to disappear completely, being subsumed into an enlarged Eastern Region.

To the railway enthusiast the West Riding became one of the last centres where steam could be regarded as dominant. The final rites were not performed until late 1967/early 1968. This illustrated volume is designed as a pictorial tribute to the last two decades of steam operation in the West Riding. It does not pretend to be a definitive history of the railways in the region, although it is hoped that the brief introductions to each chapter will at least provide the basic background.

Below:
Class B17/6 4-6-0 No 61668 *Bradford City* is seen outside Doncaster Works. Although many of the 'Sandringhams' had names associated with West Riding football teams, their normal haunts were to be found around East Anglia. Having Doncaster Works in the county ensured, therefore, that rare locomotives (for the area) could often be seen.
B. K. B. Green

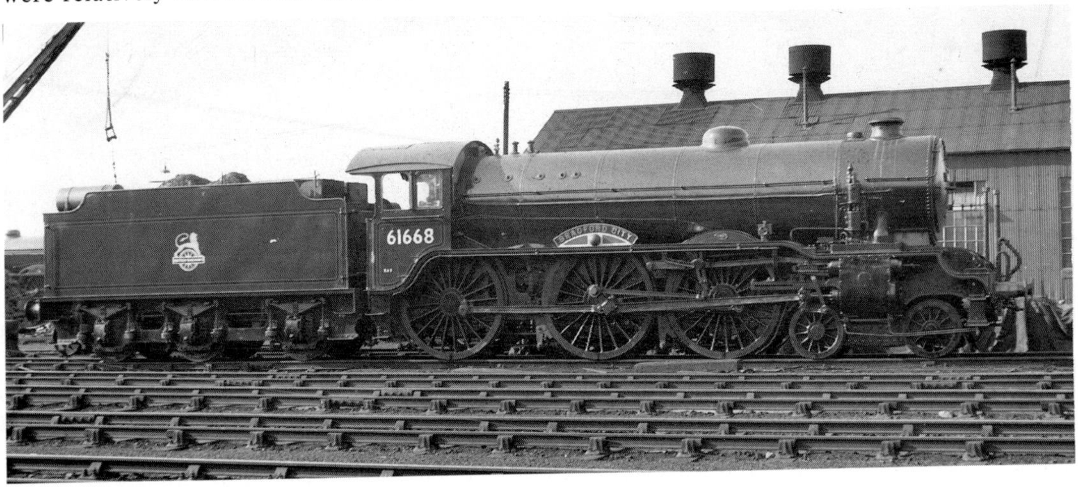

Northwest of Leeds

Just as the area to the northeast of Leeds was dominated by one railway company so too was that from the city northwestwards towards Skipton and the Pennines. Apart from a minor incursion by the Lancashire & Yorkshire Railway, which penetrated the region to join the MR at Hellifield, and the North Eastern, through its joint ownership of the Otley & Ilkley Joint, the area was a Midland fiefdom.

The first line in the area, indeed the first link to Bradford, came with the opening of the Leeds & Bradford Railway through the Aire Valley on 1 July 1846. The line was extended from Shipley to Keighley on 16 March 1847 and thence to Skipton on 28 August 1847. The line south to Colne was opened in 1848 and the associated branch from Earby to Barnoldswick on 8 February 1871. The line through Wharfedale opened in several stages — the North Eastern's Arthington-Otley section on 1 February 1865, the Midland's route from Apperley Junction to Ilkley and the joint section to Otley on 1 August 1865, the Shipley-Guiseley section on 4 December 1876 and, finally, the Ilkley-Skipton section on 1 October 1888. The Midland, thus, acquired a second through route from Skipton to the industrial West Riding, one which was to be of considerable importance as a secondary route throughout its existence.

The original Midland main line headed west from Skipton towards Lancaster although, following the opening of the line through Ingleton and Sedbergh (which was London & North Western-owned north of Ingleton) the Midland developed an interest in the growing Anglo-Scottish traffic. It was the intransigence of the LNWR that was to lead to the last great extension to the region's railway network — the construction and opening of the Settle-Carlisle line (to freight

Below:
Garsdale is the northernmost station on the Settle & Carlisle line in the West Riding. Although the main line remains open, the branch line which headed eastwards through Hawes to Northallerton is now closed. Prior to the line's closure to passenger services ex-LMS '2MT' No 41205 is seen at Garsdale having just arrived on a service from Northallerton. Services over the line were sparse, with only two through trains a day in either direction over the 40-mile line.
J. W. Armstrong

in 1875 and to passengers the following year). The Settle-Carlisle line is in the West Riding as far north as Garsdale, where a short Midland branch was constructed eastwards to link with the NER at Hawes.

Apart from the main line through the Aire Valley and the secondary route through Wharfedale, there were also three other Midland Railway branches. These were those from Keighley to Oxenhope (which opened in 1867), the short freight-only line to Yeadon (which ran eastwards from Guiseley until final closure in August 1964), and the Grassington branch (which was opened in July 1902).

The entire network of lines in the region passed to British Railways in 1948 and the traditional pattern of trains remained largely intact. There was still the 'Thames-Clyde' express which hurtled through the Aire Valley *en route* to Glasgow, the stopping services over the lines (with the exception of the line to Grassington) survived and the routes saw a great variety of freight traffic. However, as elsewhere, the process of retrenchment saw the gradual elimination of services and lines. The Worth Valley branch to Oxenhope saw passenger services withdrawn on 1 January 1962. Despite its usefulness as a diversionary route, the Skipton-Ilkley line lost its passenger services on 22 March 1965. The Barnoldswick branch succumbed on 27 September 1965. Finally, on 2 February 1970, the Skipton-Colne service was also withdrawn. Fortunately, much else survives,

Above:
Although passenger services over the Wensleydale branch from Garsdale were infrequent, the line was an important artery for freight services. 'Black 5' No 45225 is caught running from the S&C main line on to the branch. The line to Hawes was constructed by the Midland Railway whilst beyond Hawes it was a North Eastern Railway route. Freight services over the Garsdale-Hawes section were withdrawn on 16 March 1959. *J. W. Armstrong*

although even these survivors (such as the Bradford Forster Square-Shipley and Settle-Carlisle routes) only do so after years of being threatened.

Steam, despite the closure of Skipton shed in early 1967, remained active in the region until much later in the year. Indeed, the Grassington branch, courtesy of the stone traffic from the quarry at Rylstone, can lay claim to being the last branch line to see regular steam-hauled trains. The final withdrawal of these services was not, however, to be the end of steam operation in this part of the West Riding. Enthusiasts, determined not to see the destruction of the Oxenhope branch following the earlier dismantling of the lines to Queensbury, secured the branch for preservation and steam services over the branch have now been operating for more than a quarter of a century under the aegis of the Keighley & Worth Valley Railway. Further north, the Yorkshire Dales Railway Preservation Society has established a base at Embsay, on the old line from Skipton to Ilkley, and is gradually rebuilding this attractive line back towards the popular tourist centre of Bolton Abbey.

Above:
The turntable at Garsdale was one of the most exposed locations on the British Railways network and the wooden stockade was built to ensure that it could be safely operated. On 24 April 1954 'J21' No 65038 is seen being turned at Garsdale prior to hauling the last scheduled passenger service over the branch to Northallerton. The wreath commemorating the event can be seen on the front of the locomotive. Sister locomotive No 65033 was eventually to be preserved, as was the turntable, which was ultimately to find a new lease of life on the Keighley & Worth Valley Railway. *J. W. Armstrong*

Above:
A location very familiar to modern enthusiasts — the Worth Valley platforms at Keighley station — seen in April 1950 with 'N1' 0-6-2T No 69448 on a train from Halifax over the ex-Great Northern line. No 69448 was one of 13 locomotives of the class allocated in 1950 to Bradford (Hammerton Street) for use on the Queensbury Triangle services. Although two years after Nationalisation, the notice at the bottom of the ramp advertises 'To London & North Eastern & Worth Valley Trains'. *Real Photographs*

Right:
The Grassington branch was one of the last lines to open in the county. It was authorised under the Light Railways Act in 1897 and opened on 29 July 1902. Whilst nominally independent until the Grouping, the line was operated by the Midland Railway. Although passenger services were to disappear in September 1930, the line retained a sizeable business in excursion traffic for day trippers from the industrial West Riding coming to the Dales. Ex-LMS '4F' No 44041 is pictured at the branch terminus in April 1950 with a return excursion to Bradford (Forster Square). These excursions were to cease with the closure of the line beyond the quarry at Swinden in August 1969. *Real Photographs*

Below:
Another of the Great Northern incursions into traditional Midland territory was the line from Laisterdyke through Idle to Shipley. On the occasion of the SLS/MLS 'West Riding' tour of September 1953 'N1' No 69430 is seen at the weed-strewn platform at Shipley's ex-GN station. The six-mile line opened for freight services in 1874 and to passengers the following year. The link to the Midland line through the Aire Valley, which opened in late 1875, can be seen to the right of the locomotive. Whilst passenger services were withdrawn over the line as early as 2 February 1931, the route continued to see freight traffic and occasional excursion trains until the 1960s. The section from Idle to Shipley, including the link to the Midland line, was closed on 7 October 1968. Whilst much of the trackbed through Bradford has now disappeared, the ex-GN station building at Shipley survives (clearly visible from passing trains) as a tribute to the ambition (or folly) of the pre-Grouping companies.
Real Photographs

KEIGHLEY TO OXENHOPE — WEEKDAYS

H 48

DOWN																										
			B	B	B	B	B	B	B	B	B	B	B	B	B	B	B	B	B	B		B		B	B	
			Diesel	Diesel	Diesel	Diesel	Diesel	Diesel	Diesel	Diesel	Diesel	Diesel	Diesel	Diesel	Diesel	Diesel	Diesel	Diesel	Diesel	Diesel		Diesel		Diesel	Diesel	
			2 L62	2 L62	2 L62	2 L62	2 L62	2 L62	2 L62	2 L62	2 L62	2 L62	2 L62	2 L62	2 L62	2 L62	2 L62	2 L62	2 L62	2 L62	2 L62	2 L62	2 L62	2 L62	2 L62	
Mileage M	Mileage C					SO	SO			SO	SX	SO												SO	SO	
			am	am	am	am	am	am	PM	PM	PM	PM	PM	PM	PM	PM	PM	PM	PM	PM		PM		PM	PM	
0	0	KEIGHLEY dep	6 50	7 40	9 15	10 0	10 42	11 40	12 20	1 5	1 15	1 50	2 40	3 45	4 25	5 17	5 57	6 37	7 34	8 14	..	9 12	..	10 33	11 15	..
1	15	Ingrow	6 54	7 44	9 19	10 4	10 46	11 44	12 24	1 9	1 19	1 54	2 44	3 49	4 29	5 21	6 1	6 41	7 38	8 18	..	9 16	..	10 37	11 19	..
2	54	Oakworth	6 59	7 49	9 24	10 9	10 51	11 49	12 29	1 14	1 24	1 59	2 49	3 54	4 34	5 26	6 6	6 46	7 43	8 23	..	9 21	..	10 42	11 24	..
3	42	Haworth	7 3	7 53	9 28	10 13	10 55	11 53	12 33	1 18	1 28	2 3	2 53	3 58	4 38	5 30	6 10	6 50	7 47	8 27	..	9 25	..	10 46	11 28	..
4	62	OXENHOPE arr	7 6	7 56	9 31	10 16	10 58	11 56	12 36	1 21	1 31	2 6	2 56	4 1	4 41	5 33	6 13	6 53	7 50	8 30	..	9 28	..	10 49	11 31	..

OXENHOPE TO KEIGHLEY — WEEKDAYS

UP																										
					B	B	B	B	B	B	B	B	B	B	B	B	B	B	B	B	B	B	B	B	C	
					Diesel	Diesel	Diesel	Diesel	Diesel	Diesel	Diesel	Diesel	Diesel	Diesel	Diesel	Diesel	Diesel	Diesel	Diesel	Diesel	Diesel	Diesel	Diesel	Diesel	Empty Diesel Unit	
					2 L62	2 L62	2 L62	2 L62	2 L62	2 L62	2 L62	2 L62	2 L62	2 L62	2 L62	2 L62	2 L62	2 L62	2 L62	2 L62	2 L62	2 L62	2 L62	2 L62	3 L62	
Mileage M	Mileage C							SO	SO			SO	SX	SO										SO	SO	
					am	am	am	am	am	noon	PM	PM	PM	PM	PM	PM	PM	PM	PM	PM	PM	PM	PM	PM	PM	
0	0	OXENHOPE dep	..	..	7 10	8 10	9 35	10 21	11 5	12 0	12 40	1 30	1 45	2 10	3 2	4 5	4 52	5 37	6 17	6 57	7 55	8 35	9 30	10 51	11†35	..
1	20	Haworth	..	..	7 13	8 13	9 38	10 24	11 8	12 3	12 43	1 33	1 48	2 13	3 5	4 8	4 55	5 40	6 20	7 0	7 58	8 38	9 34	10 54	11c40	..
2	8	Oakworth	..	..	7 16	8 16	9 41	10 27	11 11	12 6	12 46	1 36	1 51	2 16	3 8	4 11	4 58	5 43	6 23	7 3	8 1	8 41	9 37	10 57	11 43	..
3	47	Ingrow	..	..	7 21	8 21	9 46	10 32	11 16	12 11	12 51	1 41	1 56	2 21	3 13	4 16	5 3	5 48	6 28	7 8	8 6	8 46	9 43	11 2	11c50	..
4	62	KEIGHLEY arr	..	..	7 24	8 24	9 49	10 35	11 19	12 14	12 54	1 44	1 59	2 24	3 16	4 19	5 6	5 51	6 31	7 11	8 9	8 49	9 46	11 5	11†53	..

Below:
The ex-Midland branch line from Keighley to Oxenhope again reverberates to the sound of steam as services of the Worth Valley Railway pound their way up the gradient. In October 1956, five years before BR withdrew passenger services, Fairburn-designed 2-6-4T No 42138 is seen at Oxenhope having arrived with the 1.15pm departure from Keighley. The paucity of passengers demonstrates the increasingly strained financial circumstances of branch lines such as this in the 1950s and why so many of them were to disappear.
Real Photographs

Right:
With the spire of the Norman Shaw-designed Holy Trinity prominent in the background, Class 4 2-6-0 No 43052 departs from Bingley with the 12.30pm Morecambe-Leeds service on 27 May 1961. One of the young Norman Shaw's first independent designs, Holy Trinity was later to be demolished despite being regarded as one of the architect's finest works. *John S. Whiteley*

Above:
'Black 5' No 45212 (which was later preserved) is seen approaching Skipton from the east in August 1966 with a Leeds-Heysham parcels train. The overbridge carries the ex-Midland line to Embsay Junction, where the branch to Grassington diverged from the secondary route that ran to Ilkley. By 1966 the line from Embsay Junction to Ilkley had been abandoned (although the stretch from Embsay Junction to Embsay station was eventually to form part of the preserved Yorkshire Dales Railway) and only the branch remained. In 1994 the Grassington branch still survives for the transporting of limestone from the quarry at Rylstone. *Dr L. A. Nixon*

Skipton (24G)
Allocation as at 1959

Class 2P	40586
Class 2	41327
Class 4F	43893, 43913, 43960, 43999, 44000, 44007, 44041, 44105, 44119, 44197, 44220, 44222, 44277, 44431
Class 2	46442, 46452
Class 3F	47427, 47428, 47454
Class 4	76048
Class 2	84015

Above:
Headed by 'Britannia' No 70029 *Shooting Star*, a down freight is seen at Skipton North Junction on 18 April 1967. No 70029 was one of the 'Britannias' originally allocated to the Western Region. By April 1967 the locomotive was to be based at Carlisle Kingmoor, from where she was withdrawn in December 1967. *H. Weston*

Above:
No 45593 *Kolhapur* heads the 3.15pm Bradford Forster Square-Heysham parcels train near Giggleswick on 30 September 1967. This was the locomotive's last scheduled working before withdrawal and eventual preservation.
John H. P. Hunt

Below:
On 5 September 1959 'Black 5' No 44892 is seen approaching Gargrave with the 1.52pm Leeds-Morecambe service.
R. H. Short

Above:
'Britannia' No 70039 *Sir Christopher Wren* climbs away from Settle with the LCGB 'Thames-Tyne' special on 3 June 1967. By this date No 70039 was a Kingmoor-based locomotive, having been originally allocated to the Eastern Region. Withdrawals of the 'Britannias' had already significantly reduced the number in service and *Sir Christopher Wren* was to succumb three months later in September 1967.
Ian G. Holt

Below:
The Grassington branch, kept open long after the passenger services were withdrawn to transport limestone from the quarries at Rylstone, was destined to become the last branch regularly served by steam. On 7 June 1968, barely two months before the final demise of main line steam, Carnforth-allocated BR Standard Class 4 No 75019 (one of 10 of the class to survive into 1968) is seen heading towards Skipton along the branch with a full load of limestone.
K. P. Lawrence

Right:
'Crab' No 42847 awaits departure from the ex-Midland terminus at Grassington & Threshfield with a return excursion to Manchester Victoria on 7 August 1961. The section of the branch from Rylstone to Grassington closed completely on 11 August 1969. *A. Moyes*

Below:
Having travelled over the Settle-Carlisle route, 'Black 5' No 45374 and '9F' No 92071 approach Hellifield on 3 June 1967 with a block oil train. *Ian G. Holt*

Left:
With water gushing over the tender, 'Jubilee' No 45705 *Seahorse*, departs from Hellifield with the 9.20am Manchester Victoria-Glasgow Central service on 25 July 1964. *A. W. Martin*

Left:
'Clan' Pacific No 72005 *Clan Macgregor* passes Settle Junction with a train of down empties on 1 August 1959. Allocated to Carlisle Kingmoor, along with four other members of this small class, No 72005 was the first of the English-based quintet to be withdrawn (in April 1965). *N. Fields*

Left:
On 3 August 1959 — the August Bank Holiday in the era when that day fell at the start rather than the end of the month — Stanier two-cylinder 2-6-4T No 42542 awaits departure from Hellifield with the 11.55am slow service to Carlisle.
M. Mensing

Above:
Carnforth-based BR Standard Class 4 No 75048 trundles between Cracoe and Rylstone with the morning service of limestone from Swinden lime works to Skipton on 26 April 1968. Almost 30 years on the branch survives, although diesel, rather than steam, is the order of the day. *Ian Krause*

Right:
Ivatt '2MT' No 46442 is seen departing from Hellifield with the 10am Bradford Forster Square-Heysham service on 29 June 1957. *B. K. B. Green*

Above:
A view looking west at Hellifield station sees Stanier 2-6-4T No 42278 acting as station pilot and 'Black 5' No 45268 ready to depart from the station with a southbound service. Hellifield possessed a small locomotive depot with an allocation of 15 locomotives in 1959. Visible between the two locomotives is the shed's small coaling stage. Hellifield shed was to close in 1963. *Derek Singleton*

Below:
A coke train bound for the Furness area heads away from Hellifield on 9 August 1961 with Ivatt Class 4 2-6-0 No 43113 in charge. *R. S. Greenwood*

Above:
On 8 July 1967 the unique 'Black 5' fitted with Stephenson valve gear, No 44767, approaches Clapham Junction with the Saturdays Only 10.35am Morecambe-Bradford Forster Square service. Later preserved, No 44767 is now displayed at the North Yorkshire Moors Railway. *David E. Gouldthorpe*

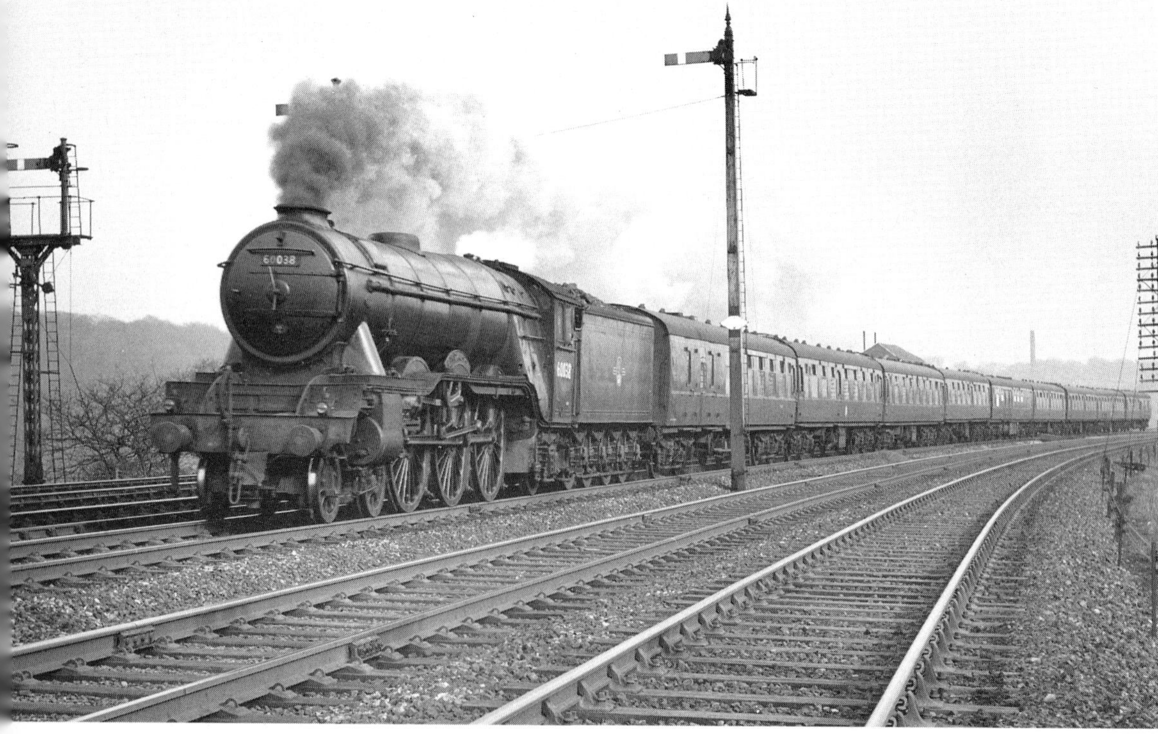

Top:
'8F' No 48394 is pictured near Hellifield with a northbound freight. *J. Davenport*

Above:
During the 1960s it became increasingly common to see ex-LNER Pacifics running over the ex-Midland line towards Skipton. Here 'A3' No 60038 *Firdaussi* is photographed on 11 March 1961 with the down 'Thames-Clyde' express between Calverley and Apperley Bridge. *A. Hobbs*

Bradford

Bradford, although situated at the westernmost extremity of the great Yorkshire coalfield at the point where the coal was closest to the surface and a centre of the early iron industry in the region (the famous ironworks of Low Moor and Bowling were both close by), was not to be served by a railway service until the opening of the Leeds & Bradford Railway on 1 July 1846. Until then, intending travellers had had to make their way by stage coach to the Manchester & Leeds line at Mirfield. The geographical position of Bradford was the primary factor in this in that the town lay at the head of a north-facing dale and the easiest approach was from the Aire Valley at Shipley — a line also adopted by the earlier Bradford Canal.

The L&BR was eventually absorbed by the Midland and the Midland station, originally named Market Street, was eventually renamed Forster Square. From this station the MR, and later the LMS and BR, operated a range of local and long-distance trains. To service the route the engine shed at Manningham (which replaced an older shed close to the terminus), one of three to serve Bradford, was opened in 1872. Apart from MR services, the station also played host to a through Bradford-Harrogate service operated by the North Eastern (later LNER) over the Otley & Ilkley Joint line.

The second company to reach Bradford was the Lancashire & Yorkshire which finally reached the town in 1850. The new station, situated less than a quarter of a mile from the original MR terminus, was located at the bottom of a steep (about 1 in 50) gradient which ran for about two miles southwards towards Low Moor. Even this gradient could not avoid the need for the 1,648yd Bowling Tunnel and other engineering works. Low Moor was the hub of the L&YR's activities in

Below:
Of all the stations in the West Riding, Bradford Exchange was, arguably, the most dramatic. With its 10 platforms and twin train shed it was a remarkable building and it is one of the greatest tragedies in the decimation of railway architecture since the mid-1960s that the building was allowed to deteriorate in the way that it did and then be demolished. Few who knew the station will ever forget the sight of trains descending the gradient from Mill Lane Junction under the lattice girders of the Bridge Street bridge. Exchange was divided between the LMS and LNER and, in the LNER half of the station, 'B1' 4-6-0 No 61267 awaits departure in May 1956 with a train for London King's Cross. In the last years of steam Exchange was to become synonymous with the last 'B1s', most notably No 61306 (later preserved).
Real Photographs

Bradford (Manningham) (55F)
Allocation as at 1959

Class 4P	41063
Class 2	41257, 41266, 41273, 41325, 41326
Class 4	42072, 42093, 42139, 42141
Class 6P5F	42702, 42762, 42770
Class 4	43016, 43030, 43070
Class 3F	43178, 43586, 43784
Class 4F	43944, 44055, 44216, 44400
Class 3F	47419
Class 2P	50795

Left:
Low Moor was the major shed in Bradford for services over the ex-L&YR lines from the city. Its allocation, until the closure of Bradford (Hammerton Street) to steam in 1958, was largely of ex-LMS types. Subsequently, a number of ex-LNER types also appeared. However, the presence of a BR 'Standard' was unusual. With the appropriately named Railway Terrace of railwaymen's cottages as a backdrop, 'Standard' 2-6-2T No 84014 gently simmers outside the shed. This particular locomotive, one of the last of the type to survive in service (being withdrawn in December 1965), was based in and around Manchester for all its operational career. Low Moor shed was to remain open until 1967 and the final withdrawal of steam from North Eastern Region metals. *Real Photographs*

Left:
On the ascent from Bradford (Exchange) the first station to be encountered on the ex-GN section, immediately after Mill Lane Junction, was St Dunstans. The station closed on 15 September 1952, although the platforms and buildings remain intact almost a decade later as 'B1' No 61383 passes with a three-coach train. Behind the signalbox on the left of the picture can be seen the ex-GN lines heading towards Queensbury. At Mill Lane Junction — the box in the middle distance — the ex-L&YR lines continued on to Bowling Junction and Halifax. *Geoff Lumb*

the area, being both a junction (with the Spen Valley branch diverging from the main route towards Manchester and, eventually, the short-lived Great Northern link to Dudley Hill) and a major locomotive shed. Low Moor was destined to become one of the last sheds in the West Riding to maintain an allocation of steam during the final run-down in 1967.

The final player in the history of Bradford railways came with the arrival of the Great Northern. The GNR opened its terminus at Adolphus Street in 1854. This was, however, only to be a temporary destination as from 1867 — following an expensive and difficult extension — the GNR diverted its services to a new joint station with the L&YR — Bradford (Exchange). The GNR was eventually to construct a network of lines in the triangle bounded by Bradford, Leeds and Wakefield as well as the branch to Shipley and the routes to Halifax and Keighley via Queensbury. Locomotive facilities were provided by a shed at Bowling (later known as Hammerton Street).

In the early years of the 20th century the Midland developed a grand plan for building a main line from Royston, on the main line south from Leeds, to Bradford through the Spen Valley to link with the Shipley-Bradford line. This line, if completed, would have shortened the MR's link to Scotland and also put Bradford on to a through main line. In the event, the line was constructed only as far as Dewsbury when World War 1 intervened and it was never completed. The result was that Bradford retained two terminus stations and was increasingly perceived as no more than a second-class railway town.

In 1948 BR inherited the almost completely intact railway network in the city. Although passenger services had been withdrawn over the Laisterdyke-Shipley line and from a number of local stations, the network bequeathed to the 'Big Four' in 1923 remained.

Inevitably, however, duplication of lines and services meant that over the next 20 years the majority of services were to succumb, leaving a rump of the lines to Halifax, Shipley and Leeds. Modernisation came early to the city; Hammerton Street was one of the first depots to be converted for the use of the new diesel multiple-units but even these could not save many of the services. Despite the arrival of the DMUs, regular steam operation continued until 1967 with a rich variety of locomotives based at Low Moor.

Ironically, in more recent years, modernisation has led to the reappearance of steam in Bradford; Forster Square is now a regular departure point now that Leeds has been electrified.

Below:
Although constructed by the L&YR, '2P' No 50636 was, by 1950, one of 11 of the class allocated to the ex-Midland shed in Bradford (Manningham). It is, therefore, close to home when pictured at Bradford (Forster Square) station in April 1950. In the background can be seen the wooden and concrete cooling towers of the city's Valley Road power station. Coal-fired, its traffic was to be one of the most important freight flows along the line from Shipley. Dating originally from 1889, Valley Road could claim to be the first municipally-owned power station in the country. Finally closed by the CEGB in the 1970s, the site has now been cleared.
Real Photographs

45205

Low Moor (56F) Allocation as at 1959

Class 2	41250, 41253, 41262, 41263
Class 4	42073, 42084, 42107, 42108, 42109, 42116, 42188, 42189, 42411, 42622, 42649, 42650
Class 4	43100
Class 3F	43570
Class 4F	44062
Class 5	44693, 44694, 44695, 44824, 44912, 44946, 44951, 44990, 45207, 45208, 45219
Class 2	46483
Class 3F	47255, 47405, 47446, 47635
Class 8F	48080, 48394, 48702
Class 3F	52413, 52461
Class B1	61020 *Gemsbok*, 60123 *Hirola*, 61039 *Steinbok*, 61049, 61230, 61383
Class J6	64170, 64203, 64226
Class J39	64791, 64796, 64801, 64817, 64872, 64886, 64903, 64907, 64919
Class J50	68895, 68908, 68912, 68922, 68923, 68932, 68933, 68943, 68944, 68969
Class WD	90333, 90711

Above left:
On 6 August 1960 the 1.59pm Saturdays Only service from Skegness to Bradford Exchange was hauled up the 1 in 42 bank between Howden Clough and Adwalton Junction by two Thompson-designed 'B1' 4-6-0s Nos 61295 and 61296. *M. Mitchell*

Below left:
Two years later, on 4 August 1962, the same train (albeit now timed to depart from Skegness at 1.57pm) is in the hands of two unfamiliar locomotives for this ex-GN line — 'Black 5' No 45200 and Mogul No 42861. *M. Mitchell*

Right:
Thompson 'B1' No 61306 heads towards Laisterdyke with the Bradford portion of the 9.55am up express for London on 30 September 1967. Note the second coach — a Pullman — in the reversed livery of pale blue and silver used on such vehicles at this date. By this time No 61306 — a Low Moor-based locomotive — was one of the last three active 'B1s' and all three were to be withdrawn on this date. Fortunately, No 61306, built by North British in 1948 and one of the first to be delivered direct to British Railways, was to be preserved. *J. B. Mounsey*

Above:
Scheduled steam-operated services between Leeds and Bradford were withdrawn on Sunday 1 October 1967. The day before saw 'Black 5' No 45428, which was also to feature the following day hauling the 2.18pm Leeds-Bradford service, pulling the 1.25pm King's Cross service. It is seen here approaching Laisterdyke, with the outskirts of Pudsey on the hillside in the distance. *J. B. Mounsey*

Left:
On Sunday 1 October 1967 the last Leeds-Bradford steam working — the through coaches off the 9.20am King's Cross-Leeds/Bradford service — was hauled by Fairburn 2-6-4T No 42152. Having just passed through Laisterdyke, the train is descending the steep gradient *en route* to Bradford Exchange. The ballast on the right indicates the formation of the Laisterdyke-Bowling Junction 'Bradford Avoiding Line'. *J. B. Mounsey*

Above:
A dramatic view looking from Laisterdyke towards the centre of Bradford which shows both how sharply the railway had to descend to reach Exchange station and how extensive the railway facilities at this point were. On 28 July 1964 Fowler 2-6-4T No 42406 climbs towards Laisterdyke with the Bradford portion of the 3.9pm service to London. Of the lines illustrated, the four on the right descended past Hammerton Street MPD towards Mill Lane Junction. The centre left roads avoided Bradford and headed towards the ex-L&YR Bradford-Halifax line at Bowling Junction and those on the extreme left served Planetrees Yard and other facilities in the Laisterdyke area. By the 1990s, apart from two running lines descending to the new Bradford Interchange and the rusting track serving a local scrapyard, all these lines have disappeared. *M. Mitchell*

Below:
With the twin arches of the trainshed at Bradford Exchange visible beyond the Bridge Street bridge, Fairburn 2-6-4T No 42283 starts the 4.18pm Sunday service through coaches to King's Cross up the 1 in 50 gradient towards Mill Lane Junction and St Dunstans on 23 July 1967.
J. B. Mounsey

Above left:
Having just passed through the 1,648yd Bowling Tunnel, south of Bradford, Fairburn 2-6-4T No 42055 approaches Low Moor with the 3.20pm Bradford Exchange-Stockport Edgeley service on 30 July 1966. *J. B. Mounsey*

Centre left:
'N1' No 69472 clatters down the 1 in 42 gradient between Howden Clough and Batley with a Bradford Exchange-Dewsbury-Wakefield local service. It is seen passing the site of Upper Batley station, which had closed to passenger services on 4 February 1952. At the date of this photograph, September 1956, the ex-GN line had only eight years to go before closure in September 1964. *Kenneth Field*

Below left:
With the signal pulled off, 'Jubilee' No 45565 *Victoria* is about to depart from Bradford Exchange with an enthusiasts' special on 5 September 1965 run on behalf of the Halifax Railfans. The train, 'South Yorkshireman No 4', was timed to depart from Bradford at 8.45am and travel via Halifax and Huddersfield to Crewe for a trip round the works. The fare was 20s (£1.00). *J. B. Mounsey*

Right:
Having just passed through Laisterdyke station, seen in the background, an unidentified 'N1' descends towards Bradford Exchange with the through coaches of an express from King's Cross. The lines to the right of the photograph formed the avoiding line to Bowling Junction. The station at Laisterdyke closed on 4 July 1966 concurrently with the closure of the line to Ardsley. *Kenneth Field*

Left:
Fairburn 2-6-4T No 42141 drifts cautiously down the gradient into Bradford Exchange with the through coaches from the 1.20pm King's Cross service on 23 July 1967. Less than a decade later this would be the location of the new Bradford Exchange station as the line under the Bridge Street bridge was abandoned and the old station demolished. *J. B. Mounsey*

Centre left:
Drighlington & Adwalton was one of a number of intermediate stations on the ex-Great Northern Laisterdyke-Ardsley/Dewsbury line. It was to lose its passenger services on 1 January 1962, although non-stop passenger services through the station were to survive until the withdrawal of passenger services over the Ardsley-Laisterdyke line on 4 July 1966. Here 'J39' No 64754 is seen stopping at the station with a local service from Bradford to Wakefield via Batley.
Kenneth Field

Below:
'N1' 0-6-2T No 69452 passes the signalbox at St Dunstans with a Wakefield-Dewsbury-Bradford Exchange local service.
Kenneth Field

Above:
The Great Northern link from Laisterdyke, past the original station at Adolphus Street (which remained as a freight depot when passenger services were diverted), to Bradford Exchange was via a deep cutting on a steeply graded (1 in 50) and curved alignment. The line was authorised in 1864 and, despite being less than a mile in length, took more than two years to complete before opening in 1867. Here Gresley-designed 'J39' No 64796 pilots 'B1' No 61296 down the gradient with an express from Cleethorpes. The lines curving away to No 64796's left allowed access from the Leeds direction on to the Queensbury route. The section from St Dunstans to City Road goods yard was to be the last part of this route to survive, being finally closed in 1972.
Kenneth Field

The Queensbury Triangle

The lines linking Bradford with Halifax and Keighley via Queensbury represented the Great Northern's efforts to reach further into both Midland and Lancashire & Yorkshire territory. Opened in stages during the 1870s and 1880s, the lines featured some of the most spectacular engineering works in the West Riding — such as Thornton viaduct, Hewenden viaduct, the tunnels at Queensbury and Lees Moor (incidentally almost half the mileage between Bradford and Holmfield was in tunnels), the triangular station at Queensbury — and well-merited the reputation amongst crews of being the Alpine line. Apart from the passenger routes, there were also the short freight-only branches to City Road in Bradford and St Pauls in Halifax. The latter line did, however, have a passenger service until 1 January 1917.

The lines, which had cost around £1 million to build, probably never fulfilled the railway's expectations and further threats to their existence came with the construction of municipal tramways in both Bradford and Halifax. Although there was a difference in gauge (Bradford's gauge was 4ft 0in and Halifax's 3ft 6in) which precluded through running, their meeting at Queensbury — the highest tram terminus in Britain — provided a more convenient form of transport than the poorly-sited station. Apart from the closure to passenger services of the St Pauls line, the station at Manchester Road (Bradford) also fell victim during World War 1.

Despite competition from trams and later buses, the service was to survive into the 1950s. The LNER timetable for the summer of 1947 records that journey times from Bradford to Halifax were around 34min whilst those to Keighley were around 47min. Neither compared particularly well with the direct routes via Low Moor or Shipley. Whilst there was considerable opposition at the time, the routes were closed to passenger services in May 1955. Freight services survived longer, although these were gradually withdrawn over the next decade with the exception of the City Road branch in Bradford, which lasted until 1972, and a short section from Halifax to the goods yard at North Bridge, which closed in April 1974. Since closure, much of the trackbed has been reclaimed and landscaped. A great deal, however, survives, most notably the viaducts at Thornton, Hewenden and Cullingworth.

Below:
A Class N1 0-6-2T takes the Halifax line at Queensbury with a two-coach train from Bradford. The road to the village served, some half mile distant, was up the hillside to the right of the train. Of note are the GN signalbox (of 40 levers) and, on the extreme left, cast-iron GNR sign. *Roy Brook*

Locomotives used over the line were predominantly ex-Great Northern designs, latterly 'N1' 0-6-2Ts based at Bradford. There was also a small subshed at Ingrow (part of which survives). Other types seen included a variety of LNER 4-6-0 designs and, after Nationalisation, both ex-LMS locomotives and ex-WD 2-8-0s also appeared. Prior to the lifting of the line through Lees Moor tunnel, experiments were undertaken using both steam and diesel locomotives on fuel emissions. This brought 'A3' Pacific No 60081 *Shotover* to the line.

The Queensbury Triangle routes are now but a memory, but the remains that survive form a remarkable tribute to the Victorian conviction that railways could reach and serve every part of the realm.

Above right:
'N1' No 69478 waits at Wilsden with a two-coach train bound for Keighley. Immediately after departing from this station the train would cross Hewenden Viaduct, one of many fine structures on this heavily engineered 'Alpine' route, before reaching the next station at Cullingworth. Note the GNR summersault signal and the number of freight wagons in the yard. Although passenger traffic over these ex-GN lines was sparse, there was much freight traffic to the many freight yards and sidings served. *Roy Brook*

Centre right:
21 May 1955 was the final day of passenger services over the Triangle lines. Amongst locomotives in use on the day was 'N1' 0-6-2T No 69467 seen at Cullingworth. The facilities at this station were remarkable considering the size of the settlement served; ironically, since the railway closed, Cullingworth has expanded considerably. Freight services continued to the goods yard for a further eight years. *Roy Brook.*

Below right:
The afternoon train from Keighley to Halifax is seen at Wilsden hauled by Ivatt 'N1' No 69430. This was the prototype of this ex-GNR class of 0-6-2Ts and dated from 1907. The date of the photograph was June 1954, just under a year before the line lost its passenger services (in May 1955). Wilsden station was some half a mile from Harecroft — the nearest settlement — and some two miles from the village it purported to serve; factors which, no doubt, contributed to eventual closure.
G. B. Blacklock

Above:
The Queensbury Triangle lines were heavily engineered with much of the route either in tunnels or on viaducts. The costs of construction were immense and it is unlikely that the long-suffering shareholders of either the GNR or LNER saw much of a return. One of the ubiquitous 'N1s' which served the line for many years emerges from one of the line's many tunnels. *Roy Brook*

Table 94 **BRADFORD, KEIGHLEY, and HALIFAX (via Queensbury)**

Week Days / **Sundays**

Miles		p.m A	a.m B	a.m A		a.m A	a.m A	a.m B	a.m A		p.m B	p.m A	a.m B		a.m A	p.m A	p.m B	p.m B		p.m A	p.m A		p.m	p.m A	p.m B	p.m A	Sun	Sun	Sun
	1 London (King's Cross) dep	10J40	..	..	..	..	..	..	4 25	..	..	..	8R45	..	10R10	..	12S35	..	..	1R10	1R25	..	..	4R 0	..	6RT5	..	..	..
—	**Bradford** (Exchange) ... dep	5a45	5 55	6 30	..	7 15	7 54	9 3	10 8	..	12 10	12 50	1p30	..	3p30	4 38	5 15	5 45	..	6 0	6 46	..	..	9 15	10 27	11 20	..	..	..
½	St. Dunstan's	5 49	5 58	6Y35	..	7 20	7 58	9 6	10 11	..	12 13	12 53	1Z36	..	3 34	4 41	5 18	5 48	..	..	6 49	..	..	9 19	..	..	..	..	..
1¼	Horton Park	5 53	[illegible]	6 39	..	7 24	8 2	9 10	10 15	..	12 17	12 57	1 40	..	3 38	4 45	5 22	5 52	..	6 6	6 53	..	..	..	..	..	..	..	..
2¼	Great Horton	5 56	[illegible]	6 42	..	7 27	8 5	9 13	10 18	..	12 20	1 0	1 43	..	3 41	4 48	5 25	5 55	..	6 9	6 56	..	..	9 25	10 34	..	..	..	..
3½	Clayton	6 0	6 12	6 46	..	7 31	8 9	9 17	10 22	..	12 24	1 4	1 47	..	3 45	4 52	5 29	5 59	..	6 13	7 0	..	..	9 29	10 38	..	..	..	..
4½	**Queensbury** ... arr	6 4	[illegible]	6 50	..	7 35	8 13	9 21	10 26	..	12 28	1 8	1 51	..	3 49	4 56	5 33	6 3	..	6 17	7 4	..	..	9 33	10 42	..	..	..	..
—	Queensbury ... dep	..	6 1[illegible]	6N55	..	..	8N18	9 25	10N35	..	12 29	..	1 52	..	3N54	5N 0	5 37	6 7	..	..	..	..	..	..	10 49	..	..	..	..
6½	Thornton	..	6 2[illegible]	6 59	..	..	8 22	9 29	10 39	..	12 33	..	1 56	..	3 58	5 4	5 41	6 11	..	..	..	..	..	..	10 53	..	..	..	..
7½	Denholme	..	6 2[illegible]	7 2	..	..	8 25	9 32	10 42	..	12 36	..	1 59	..	4 1	5 7	5 44	6 14	..	..	..	..	..	..	10 56	..	..	..	..
8¾	Wilsden	..	6 2[illegible]	7 5	..	..	8 28	9 35	10 45	..	12 39	..	2 2	..	4 4	5 10	5 47	6 17	..	..	..	..	..	..	10 59	..	..	..	..
9¾	Cullingworth	..	6 3[illegible]	7 9	..	..	8 31	9 38	10 48	..	12 42	..	2 5	..	4 7	5 13	5 50	6 20	..	..	..	..	..	..	11 2	..	..	..	..
12½	Ingrow	..	6 39	7 15	..	..	8 38	9 45	10 55	..	12 49	..	2 12	..	4 14	5 20	5 57	6 27	..	..	..	..	..	..	11 9	..	..	..	..
13½	**Keighley** ... arr	..	6 42	7 19	..	..	8 41	9 48	10 58	..	12 52	..	2 15	..	4 17	5 23	6 0	6 30	..	..	..	..	..	..	11 12	..	..	..	..
—	**Queensbury** ... dep	6 7	..	6 58	..	7 38	8 15	9N26	10 34	..	12N32	1 15	..	..	3 52	5 4	5N37	..	..	6 18	7 8	..	8 8	9 37	10N51	..	..	..	..
7	Holmfield	6 11	..	7 2	..	7 42	8 19	9 30	10 38	..	12 36	1 19	..	..	3 56	5 10	5 41	..	..	6 22	7 12	..	8 12	9 41	10 55	..	..	..	..
7½	Ovenden	6 13	..	7 4	..	7 44	8 21	9 32	10 40	..	12 38	1 21	..	..	3 58	5 12	5 43	..	..	6 24	7 14	..	8 14	9 43	10 57	..	..	..	..
9	**Halifax** (North Bridge)	6 17	..	7 8	..	7 48	8 25	9 36	10 44	..	12 42	1 25	..	..	4 2	5 16	5 47	..	..	6 28	7 18	..	8 18	9 47	11 1	..	..	..	..
9½	" (Old) ... arr	6 19	..	7 10	..	7 50	8 27	9 38	10 46	..	12 44	1 27	..	..	4 4	5 18	5 49	..	..	6 30	7 20	..	8 20	9 49	11 3	11 43	..	..	..

Week Days / **Sundays**

Miles		a.m B	a.m B	a.m B		a.m A	a.m A	a.m B		p.m A	p.m B		p.m A		p.m B	p.m B		p.m B	p.m A	p.m A		p.m B	p.m B	p.m A		p.m A		Sun	Sun p.m A	Sun
—	**Halifax** (Old) ... dep	6N35	..	7N50	..	8 20	9 5	10N12	..	12 3	..	..	1 17	..	..	3N35	..	4N42	5 10	5 43	..	..	..	7 50	..	10 25	..	..	4 18	..
½	" (North Bridge)	6 38	..	7 53	..	8 23	9 8	10 15	..	12 6	..	..	1 20	..	..	3 38	..	4 44	5 13	5 46	..	..	..	7 53	..	10 28	..	..	..	..
2	Ovenden	6 42	..	7 57	..	8 27	9 12	10 19	..	12 10	..	..	1 24	..	..	3 42	..	4 48	5 17	5 50	..	..	..	7 57	..	10 32	..	..	..	..
2¾	Holmfield	6 45	..	8 0	..	8 30	9 15	10 22	..	12 13	..	..	1 27	..	..	3 45	..	4 51	5 20	5 53	..	..	..	8 0	..	10 35	..	..	..	..
5	**Queensbury** ... arr	6 51	..	8 6	..	8 36	9 21	10 28	..	12 19	..	..	1 33	..	..	3 51	..	4 57	5 26	5 59	..	..	..	8 6	..	10 41	..	..	..	..
—	Mls **Keighley** ... dep	6 25	7 5	7 3[illegible]	..	..	8N52	10 1	..	11N50	12 42	..	..	..	1 41	3 18	..	4 28	4N55	..	..	5 46	6 31	7N27	..	10N15	..	..	..	..
—	1 Ingrow	6 31	7 11	7 43	..	..	8 58	10 7	..	11 56	12 48	..	..	..	1 47	3 24	..	4 34	5 1	..	..	5 52	6 37	7 33	..	10 21	..	..	..	..
—	3½ Cullingworth	6 39	7 19	7 51	..	..	9 6	10 15	..	12 4	12 56	..	..	..	1 55	3 32	..	4 42	5 9	..	..	6 1	6 45	7 41	..	10 29	..	..	..	..
—	4¾ Wilsden	6 43	7 23	7 55	..	..	9 10	10 19	..	12 8	1 0	..	..	..	1 59	3 36	..	4 46	5 13	..	..	6 5	6 49	7 45	..	10 34	..	..	..	..
—	6 Denholme	6 46	7 26	7 58	..	..	9 13	10 22	..	12 11	1 3	..	..	..	2 2	3 39	..	4 49	5 16	..	..	6 8	6 52	7 48	..	10 37	..	..	..	..
—	7½ Thornton	6 50	7 30	8 2	..	..	9 17	10 26	..	12 15	1 7	..	..	..	2 6	3 43	..	4 53	5 20	..	..	6 12	6 56	7 52	..	10 41	..	..	..	..
—	8¾ **Queensbury** ... arr	6 53	7 33	8 5	..	..	9 20	10 29	..	12 18	1 10	..	..	..	2 9	3 46	..	4 56	5 23	..	..	6 15	6 59	7 55	..	10 44	..	..	..	..
—	Queensbury ... dep	6 59	7 34	8 10	..	8 37	9 25	10 32	..	12 22	1 16	..	1 35	..	2 11	3 56	..	5 3	5 27	6 0	..	6 17	7 7	8 9	..	10 50	..	..	..	..
6	Clayton	7 2	7 37	8 13	..	8 40	9 28	10 35	..	12 25	1 19	..	1 38	..	2 14	3 59	..	5 7	5 30	6 3	..	6 20	7 10	8 12	..	10 53	..	..	..	..
7¼	Great Horton	7 5	7 40	8 16	..	8 43	..	10 38	..	12 28	1 22	..	1 41	..	2 17	4 2	..	5 10	5 33	6 6	..	6 23	7 13	8 15	..	10 56	..	..	..	..
7¾	Horton Park	7 7	7 42	8 18	..	8 45	..	10 40	..	12 30	1 24	..	1 43	..	2 19	4 5	..	5 12	5 35	6 8	..	6 25	7 15	8 17	..	..	..	..	..	..
9	St. Dunstan's	7 11	7 46	8 22	..	8 49	..	10 44	..	12 34	1 28	..	1 47	..	2 23	4 9	..	5 16	5 39	6 12	..	6 30	7 19	8 21	..	..	..	..	..	..
9½	**Bradford** (Exchange) .. arr	7 14	7 49	8 25	..	8 52	9 37	10 47	..	12 37	1 31	..	1 50	..	2 26	4 12	..	5 19	5 42	6 15	..	6 35	7 22	8 24	..	11 4	..	..	4 40	..
204½	1 **London** (King's Cross) arr	12R12	..	..	..	1R45	2R45	5HR18	..	7SR15	..	..	..	..	7R46	..	..	..	..	..	..	2a49	..	..	..	..	..	..	9 30	..

A Through Train between Bradford and Halifax.
a a.m.
B Through Train between Bradford and Keighley.
E Except Sats.
H Via Holbeck. Arr. 4 35 p.m on Fridays and Saturdays.
J Except Saturdays. Dep. 10 55 p.m. on Fridays and 11 0 p.m. on Sundays.
N Through Trains between Halifax and Keighley.
p p.m.
R Restaurant Car.
S Saturdays only.
T Dep. 6·10 p.m. on Fridays.
Y Arr. 3 mins. *earlier*
Z Arr. 4 mins. *earlier*

York

For around 150 years York has been one of the premier railway centres of Britain and a magnet for railway enthusiasts — a role that it maintains to this day as the home of the National Railway Museum.

The first railway services to the city commenced operations, courtesy of the York & North Midland, in May 1839. This was followed by the Great North of England in March 1841. Further routes followed to Scarborough (in July 1845), to Market Weighton (in October 1847), to Harrogate (in October 1848), to Selby (1871 — the former, now closed, East Coast main line), the Foss Islands goods branch (in 1880) and, lastly, the Derwent Valley Railway in 1913. With the exception of the independent Derwent Valley (which remained aloof from the Grouping and Nationalisation) all the lines were eventually to form part of the North Eastern (later London & North Eastern) Railway. Despite this, it was possible to see locomotives from several other pre-Grouping companies in the city — resulting in the provision, at one time, of locomotive facilities for several other companies in the city, such as the Midland Railway.

The original station, opened in 1839, was situated within the city walls, but this was soon incapable of accommodating the traffic and it was considerably extended, following a design by G. T. Andrews, in 1841. This station was itself to be replaced in the 1870s by the dramatic curved lines of the station, designed by Thomas Prosser, that remains today. The platforms of the old station survived until the mid-1960s when they were demolished to make way for an extension to the Hudson House office complex;

Below:
'V2' No 60889 heads a down freight formed of 12-ton ventilated vans over the Holgate Bridge Junction-Severus line avoiding York station on 22 May 1959. In the background can be seen a rake of cattle wagons — a form of traffic that has long since ceased to be transported by rail — in amongst many others on the wagon works sidings.
Brian Morrison

the (extended) block designed by Andrews, however, survives.

York emerged relatively unscathed from the closures of the Beeching era, with only the line to Market Weighton closing (on 29 November 1965). More recently, however, the old East Coast main line was replaced by the Selby Diversion and the Foss Islands branch closed (in 1989). The independent Derwent Valley has also finally closed, although part has been subsequently taken over by a preservation society.

York was also the home of the York & North Midland's locomotive department and this resulted in the construction of the Queen Street Works in the early 1840s. Although only relatively few locomotives were constructed there — the Y&NM bought most of its locomotives from outside suppliers — the site expanded considerably. However, the site was confined and allowed little room for expansion. Thus, the decision was made to transfer activity to Darlington, and York Works closed in 1905. The buildings were, however, to survive and when, in the early 1920s, the NER decided to establish a museum, Queen Street became its base. Passing through the LNER and the British Transport Commission, the museum closed only in 1973 following the decision to make York the home of the National Railway Museum. The new museum, based in the old North Shed, opened in 1975. Following further expansion and reconstruction, the NRM remains one of the most popular tourist attractions in the region.

Inevitably as a result of its location as a junction on the East Coast main line, York has seen many of the top-link steam locomotives passing through, most notably the various Pacific designs of the East Coast companies; whilst its sheds offered accommodation to a wide range of designs until York North lost its final allocation of steam locomotives in June 1967. Although that year witnessed the final withdrawal of steam in the area, it was not to be the end of the story. With the return to steam on the main line in the early 1970s, York was a natural base for such services, and steam-hauled trains reappeared on the lines to Scarborough and to Harrogate. There was also a brief period when the Derwent Valley reintroduced steam passenger services, although these did not prove successful.

With the revamped National Railway Museum the city retains much of steam interest into the 1990s.

Below:
With the dramatic lines of York station in the background, 'A3' Pacific No 60050 *Persimmon*, fitted with a double chimney, hauls a southbound Newcastle-King's Cross express past Holgate Bridge Junction on 22 May 1959. Above the locomotive can be seen one of the roundhouses at York South shed, which, by this date, was coming to the end of its life. *Brian Morrison*

Top:
'J25' No 65698 is seen stored — notice the chimney — outside one of the roundhouses at York South on 2 May 1959. At this date York South was a sub-shed of York North (50A) and comprised three basic elements: the roofless roundhouse (seen here) erected originally in 1864; a second roundhouse (just visible to the right of the locomotive); and a three-road straight shed. A third roundhouse, destroyed by fire, was demolished in the 1920s. York South was closed in May 1961 and demolished two years later.
Brian Morrison

Above:
'K3' No 61902 heads south through Selby with a train of vans for Hull on 22 May 1959. Designed by Sir Nigel Gresley, 193 of the 'K3' 2-6-0s were built after 1924, although one (No 61863) was later rebuilt by Thompson. At this time, No 61902 was based at Hull (Dairycoates). *Brian Morrison*

Top:
Departmental locomotive No 55 (ex-No 68091) was the last survivor of a class of five 0-4-0Ts designed for dock work on the North Eastern Railway by Worsdell and built in 1890. Two of the type survived at Nationalisation, although sister locomotive No 8090 was scrapped in 1948. No 55 was to survive as shunter at York, where it is seen in its own shed, until 1956. *Brian Morrison*

Above:
Although now bypassed by the East Coast main line, Selby was, throughout the steam era, an important junction between the ECML and lines towards Hull, Leeds and Market Weighton. Seen in the down platform at Selby station in April 1953, 'B1' No 61388 is heading a Wakefield-York service. From Selby the train will take the section of ECML that was to be closed completely after the construction of the Selby Diversion. *Real Photographs*

Above:
With a clutch of youthful spotters standing at the platform end, 'Black 5' No 44981 departs from York station with a southbound express from Newcastle to Birmingham on 21 May 1959. At this time the locomotive was based at the ex-Midland Railway shed at Bournville (21B) near Birmingham and so the locomotive was working a return trip back to its home district. *Brian Morrison*

Right:
Situated just to the southeast of the station, Selby shed housed a variety of ex-LNER designs, later supplemented by a number of Ivatt 2-6-0s and an odd 'Jinty'. Seen in the shed on 30 August 1954 is 'D20' No 62374, one of a number of this North Eastern design to be based here. A total of 60 of the class were constructed between 1899 and 1907, with the last being withdrawn in 1957. Although in steam at the time of this photograph, No 62374 was not to last much longer, being withdrawn later the same year. *Brian Morrison*

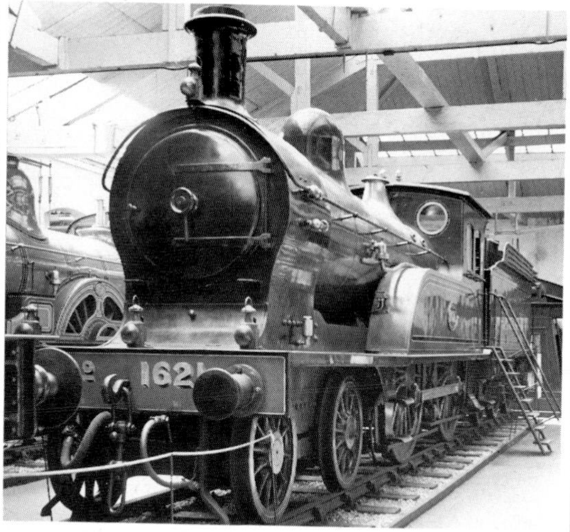

Left and centre left:
For visitors to York in the 1950s and 1960s the day was not complete without a trip to the old Railway Museum. Established initially by the LNER the museum had passed to the British Transport Commission on Nationalisation. Locomotives and other exhibits were housed in the former Queen Street workshops and, inevitably, the collection was biased towards exhibits from the constituent companies of the LNER. These included 'D17' 4-4-0 No 1621 (withdrawn in 1945) ...

... and ex-NER 2-2-4T No 66 *Aerolite*. The two locomotives are seen in the Queen Street building. This museum closed in 1973 and the exhibits were transferred to the new National Railway Museum established in the former York North shed. No 66 dated originally from 1869 as a Fletcher-built 2-2-2WT. It was rebuilt as a 4-2-2T in 1892 and again, into its present form, in 1902. Latterly used primarily to haul the directors' saloon, the locomotive was withdrawn in 1933 and preserved. *Brian Morrison (both)*

Below:
Raven 'B16' 4-6-0 No 61428 is seen at York South shed on 26 May 1959. By this date withdrawal of these ex-NER locomotives had started and the last was to succumb in 1964.
Brian Morrison

Right:
Shorn of its coupling rods, 'K1/1' No 61997 *MacCailin Mor* makes a sad sight at York North shed on 30 August 1952 whilst awaiting overhaul. This Scottish Region locomotive was rebuilt from a Gresley-designed 'K4' in 1945 to a specification produced by Gresley's successor Thompson. As such it was to form the prototype of Peppercorn's design of 2-6-0, the 'K1', introduced in 1949. Despite appearances, No 61997 was to remain in service for a further decade, before withdrawal in late 1961. *Brian Morrison*

Below:
'9F' 2-10-0 No 92177, then allocated to Doncaster, looks in need of a repaint as it heads south past York South shed with a freight on 22 May 1959. *Brian Morrison*

Above:
'A3' Pacific No 60513 *Dante* departs from York on 22 May 1959 with a southbound service from Tyne Commission Quay. The train would be conveying passengers who had arrived on Tyneside on the steamer service from Scandinavia. *Brian Morrison*

Below:
An impressive line-up at the south end of York station on 21 May 1959 sees 'Jubilee' No 45719 *Glorious*, then allocated to Bank Hall, departing with an express for Liverpool. Also visible are 'B16' No 61421 and 'Jinty' 0-6-0T No 47556, both of which were allocated to York. *Brian Morrison*

Top:
Ex-NER 'B16/2' 4-6-0 No 61435 is pictured passing Dringhouses marshalling yard south of York station with a Class 7 freight from York to Hull via Church Fenton. Dringhouses, which possessed both up and down yards, dated originally from the end of World War 1. Modernised in the early 1960s, the yard could claim in 1962 to be the first marshalling yard in the country to deal exclusively with fully-fitted freight trains. Changing traffic patterns, and the gradual loss of freight, however meant that the yard was to cease operation by the mid-1980s.
P. J. Lynch

Above:
Class A1/1 No 60113 *Great Northern* is caught underneath the gracefully-curved train shed at York with a southbound express on 29 August 1954. This particular locomotive, originally Great Northern No 1470 and LNER 4470 (until renumbered 113), was the first Pacific designed by Gresley and entered service in 1922. It was rebuilt by Edward Thompson in 1945 as the prototype for the later 'A1s' designed by Peppercorn. The rebuilding work included the replacement of the inside Gresley valve gear by Walschaerts and the provision of an 'A4' boiler. The result of the work was to increase the locomotive's boiler pressure from 180 to 250psi with an improved tractive effort of 37,397lb. *Brian Morrison*

Northeast of Leeds

To the northeast of Leeds, in the area bounded by Harrogate, York and Church Fenton, the railways were, eventually, almost the private fiefdom of the North Eastern Railway.

The first section of line, linking York with the Leeds & Selby Railway at Milford, opened in 1839. This was the York & North Midland, which was soon further extended to Normanton. The next phase of railway development occurred after the railway mania and by 1850 the routes from Church Fenton to Harrogate, York to Starbeck and from Leeds, via Starbeck, towards Ripon — the Leeds Northern — were all operational. The first station in Harrogate, served by trains from Church Fenton which ran over the dramatic Crimple viaduct, was Brunswick, but this was replaced in 1862 by a new station which was also served by trains from Leeds via a new connection at Crimple. Also in 1862 the branch line to Pateley Bridge was opened. This was followed later in the 1860s by the construction of a line from Arthington, through the Wharfe valley, to join the Midland's route to Ilkley. The section of this line from Otley to Ilkley was one of many joint lines in the West Riding; this time being jointly controlled by the MR and NER. Finally, in the 1860s the NER constructed a line from Church Fenton to Micklefield which shortened the direct Leeds-York distance.

This was not the end of railway construction in this relatively rural area; in 1876 a direct line from Cross Gates to Wetherby was opened, to be followed in 1905 by the construction of a south-west line in Wetherby to allow for a Leeds-Harrogate service. However, the rural nature of the area led to the first closure the same year, when Sutton station lost its passenger services.

Dominated by the NER and later by the LNER, the area witnessed relatively few changes before Nationalisation. However, the

Below:
A single-coach train is seen in April 1950 at the terminus of the attractive ex-North Eastern Railway branch to Pateley Bridge in the Nidd Valley. Three return services from Harrogate were operated over the 15-mile branch, with a fourth on Saturdays. The journey took just over 30min with stops at five intermediate stations. Passenger services over the branch from Ripley Valley Junction were to be withdrawn from 2 April 1951 with freight services succumbing on 2 November 1964. The stone-built station building, with its stepped gable ends, however, survives. Whilst Pateley Bridge was the terminus of the NER branch, there was a link through the town to connect with the independent Nidd Valley Light Railway which ran passenger services through the dale to Lofthouse-in-Nidderdale until January 1930.
Real Photographs

Pateley Bridge line was not to survive for long; passenger services were withdrawn in 1951. (In Pateley Bridge the branch was physically connected to the Nidd Valley Light Railway, which had lost its passenger services in 1930 and which was closed throughout in 1936.) The remaining services were to survive until the Beeching era. The lines from Church Fenton to Cross Gates and Harrogate — despite serving places like Tadcaster and Wetherby — were closed in 1964. The line from Arthington westwards succumbed in 1965 and even the old Leeds Northern main line from Starbeck through Ripon to Northallerton closed in 1967. This left the rump of the network as the main line from Micklefield to York and the York-Harrogate-Leeds (via Horsforth) routes.

Inevitably, ex-NER and ex-LNER types dominated the local railway scene. There was only one shed in the area — Starbeck — which was a relatively early casualty, being closed in September 1959. Its locomotive allocation was transferred to a variety of sheds, including York, Hull Dairycoates, Mirfield and Wakefield.

Above:
Starbeck, situated to the east of Harrogate, was, until the closure of the main line through Ripon, an important railway junction. Pictured looking southeastwards from the station, Gresley-designed 'J39' No 64861 waits for a road with a freight for sorting at the sidings. Visible beyond the crossing is Starbeck shed (50D). The line to Knaresborough and York heads to the left of the shed, whilst, to the right, a line headed south to connect with the Leeds-Harrogate line at Pannal. This route had been closed completely on 26 June 1951, although a link was retained thereafter at Starbeck to serve a steel terminal. Starbeck shed was to close in 1959.
Kenneth Field

Starbeck (50D)
Allocation as at 1959

Class 4	42477, 42553, 42639
Class 3F	47438, 47462, 47581
Class B16	61478
Class D49	62727 *The Quorn*, 62738 *The Zetland*, 62753 *The Belvoir*, 62759 *The Craven*, 62763 *The Fitzwilliam*, 62765 *The Goathland*
Class J39	64706, 64818, 64821, 64845, 64847, 64855, 64857, 64859, 64861, 64866, 64942, 64944
Class J25	65726
Class WD	90044, 90054, 90457, 90518

Table 117 CHURCH FENTON, HARROGATE, WETHERBY, and LEEDS

Week Days only

Miles	Station	a.m	a.m		a.m		a.m		a.m		a.m		a.m		a.m		p.m		a.m		p.m	p.m.		p.m	p.m	p.m		p.m		p.m	
					X				X						S		S		S		S										
	104 HULL ... dep	..	..	..	..	..	..	..	..	..	..	..	8 55	..	..	..	..	..	..	..	..	..	..	..	4 0	..	..	..	..	..	..
	104 SELBY ... "	..	..	..	..	..	..	..	..	..	..	..	10 0	..	..	..	..	..	..	..	..	..	..	..	5 10	..	..	..	..	..	..
	113 YORK 116 ... "	..	..	..	..	..	6 40	..	..	..	..	..	1015	..	..	..	..	..	1040	..	3 10	..	..	..	5 12	..	..	..	..	..	..
—	Church Fenton ... dep	..	..	..	..	..	7 35	..	..	..	..	..	1039	..	..	..	..	..	1 30	..	3 45	..	..	..	5 45	..	..	..	..	..	..
4¼	Tadcaster ...	..	..	..	..	..	7 43	..	..	..	..	..	1048	..	..	..	..	..	1 38	..	3 53	..	..	..	5 54	..	..	..	..	..	..
6¾	Newton Kyme ...	..	..	..	..	..	7 49	..	..	..	..	..	1052	..	..	..	..	..	1 42	..	3 59	..	..	..	5 59	..	..	..	..	..	..
8¼	Thorp Arch **A** ...	..	..	..	..	..	7 54	..	..	..	..	..	1056	..	..	..	..	..	1 46	..	4 3	..	..	..	6 5	..	..	..	..	..	..
11¼	Wetherby ... arr	..	..	..	..	..	8 5	..	..	..	..	..	11 2	..	..	..	..	..	1 52	..	4 9	..	..	..	6 11	..	..	..	..	..	..
—	Wetherby ... dep	..	..	..	..	..	..	..	8 15	..	..	..	..	..	1110	..	..	..	..	..	..	4 18	..	..	..	6 16	..	8 3	..	9 40	..
14	Spofforth ...	..	..	..	..	..	..	..	8 21	..	..	..	..	..	1116	..	..	..	..	..	..	4 24	..	..	..	6 22	..	..	..	9 46	..
19	**Harrogate** ... arr	..	..	..	..	..	..	..	8 32	..	..	..	..	..	1127	..	..	..	..	..	..	4 35	..	..	..	6 33	..	8 18	..	9 57	..
—	Mls **Harrogate** ... dep	6 39	..	..	7 37	..	..	..	..	..	8 10	..	..	..	..	..	1230	..	..	..	..	..	..	4 40	..	..	..	..	..	..	..
—	5 Spofforth ...	6 47	..	..	7 45	..	..	..	..	..	8 18	..	..	..	..	..	1238	..	..	..	..	..	..	4 48	..	..	..	..	..	..	..
—	7¾ Wetherby ... arr	6 52	..	..	7 51	..	..	..	..	..	8 26	..	—	..	..	..	1243	..	..	..	..	..	..	4 53	..	..	..	..	..	..	..
—	Wetherby ... dep	6 53	7 45	..	..	..	8 10	..	..	..	8 33	..	11 3	..	..	..	1253	..	1 53	..	4 10	..	..	4 56	6 13	..	..	..	..	..	..
13	Collingham Bridge ...	6 57	7 49	..	..	..	8 14	..	..	..	8 37	..	11 7	..	..	..	1257	..	1 57	..	4 15	..	..	5 0	6 18	..	..	..	..	..	..
15¼	Bardsey ...	7 2	7 54	..	..	..	8 19	..	..	..	8 42	..	1112	..	..	..	1 2	..	2 2	..	4 20	..	..	5 5	6 23	..	..	..	..	..	..
17¼	Thorner ...	7 8	8 0	..	..	..	8 25	..	..	..	8 48	..	1118	..	..	..	1 8	..	2 8	..	4 27	..	..	5 11	6 30	..	..	..	..	..	..
19¼	Scholes ...	7 14	8 6	..	..	..	8 31	..	..	..	8 54	..	1124	..	..	..	1 14	..	2 14	..	4 34	..	..	5 17	6 37	..	..	..	..	..	..
20¾	Penda's Way ...	7 17	8 9	..	..	..	8 34	..	..	..	8 57	..	1128	..	..	..	1 17	..	2 17	..	4 38	..	..	5 20	6 40	..	..	..	..	..	..
21¾	Cross Gates ...	7 20	8 12	..	..	..	8 39	..	..	..	9 0	..	1133	..	..	..	1 20	..	2 20	..	4 42	..	..	5 23	6 43	..	..	..	..	..	..
23¼	Osmondthorpe ...	7 24	8 16	..	..	..	..	..	..	..	9 4	..	1137	..	..	..	1 24	..	2 24	..	4 46	..	..	5 30	6 47	..	..	..	..	..	..
25¾	**Leeds** {Marsh Lane ...	7 29	8 21	..	..	..	..	..	..	..	9 9	..	1142	..	..	..	1 29	..	2 29	..	4 51	..	..	5 35	6 52	..	..	..	..	..	..
26	**Leeds** {City ... arr	7 32	8 24	..	..	..	8 43	..	..	..	9 12	..	1145	..	..	..	1 32	..	2 32	..	4 54	..	..	5 39	6 55	..	..	..	..	..	..

Week Days only

Miles	Station	a.m	a.m		a.m		a.m	a.m	a.m					p.m				p.m		p.m		p.m.		p.m			p.m		p.m		p.m
					X				X		S			S	S	S															
—	**Leeds** {City ... dep	..	6 32	..	..	..	7 17	..	..	..	10 30	..	..	..	12 10	1 28	..	3 50	..	..	..	4 31	..	5 35	..	..	6 33	..	7 35	..	9 [illegible]
¾	**Leeds** {Marsh Lane ...	..	6 35	..	..	..	7 20	..	..	..	10 33	..	..	..	12 13	1 31	..	..	..	..	..	4 34	..	5 38	..	..	6 36	..	..	..	9 [illegible]
2¾	Osmondthorpe ...	..	6 40	..	..	..	7 26	..	..	..	10 38	..	..	..	12 18	1 36	..	..	..	..	..	4 39	..	5 43	..	..	6 42	..	..	..	9 [illegible]
4¼	Cross Gates ...	..	6 45	..	..	..	7 31	..	..	..	10 43	..	..	..	12 23	1 41	..	..	..	..	..	4 44	..	5 48	..	..	6 48	..	..	..	9 [illegible]
5¼	Penda's Way ...	..	6 48	..	..	..	7 34	..	..	..	10 46	..	..	..	12 26	1 44	..	..	..	..	..	4 47	..	5 51	..	..	6 51	..	..	..	9 [illegible]
6¾	Scholes ...	..	6 52	..	..	..	7 38	..	..	..	10 50	..	..	..	12 30	1 48	..	..	..	..	..	4 51	..	5 55	..	..	6 55	..	..	..	9 [illegible]
8¾	Thorner ...	..	6 57	..	..	..	7 43	..	..	..	10 55	..	..	..	12 35	1 53	..	..	..	..	..	4 55	..	6 0	..	..	7 0	..	..	..	9 [illegible]
10¾	Bardsey ...	..	7 2	..	..	..	7 48	..	..	..	11 0	..	..	..	12 40	1 58	..	..	..	..	..	5 1	..	6 4	..	..	7 5	..	..	..	9 [illegible]
13	Collingham Bridge ...	..	7 7	..	..	..	7 53	..	..	..	11 5	..	..	..	12 45	2 3	..	..	..	..	..	5 6	..	6 10	..	..	7 10	..	..	..	9 [illegible]
14¾	Wetherby ... arr	..	7 11	..	..	..	7 56	..	..	..	11 8	..	..	..	12 48	2 6	..	4 17	..	..	..	5 9	..	6 14	..	..	7 13	..	8 2	..	9 [illegible]
—	Wetherby ... dep	..	..	..	..	..	..	..	8 15	..	11 10	..	..	..	..	..	..	4 18	..	..	..	..	..	6 16	..	..	..	..	8 3	..	9 [illegible]
17½	Spofforth ...	..	..	..	..	..	..	..	8 21	..	11 16	..	..	..	..	..	..	4 24	..	..	..	..	..	6 22	..	..	..	..	..	..	9 [illegible]
22½	**Harrogate** ... arr	..	..	..	..	..	..	..	8 32	..	11 27	..	..	..	..	..	..	4 35	..	..	..	..	..	6 33	..	..	..	..	8 18	..	9 [illegible]
—	Mls **Harrogate** ... dep	6 39	..	..	7 37	..	..	8 10	..	..	..	..	..	1230	..	..	..	..	..	4 40	..	..	..	..	..	..	..	..	..	..	..
—	5 Spofforth ...	6 47	..	..	7 45	..	..	8 18	..	..	..	..	..	1238	..	..	..	..	..	4 48	..	..	..	..	..	..	..	..	..	..	..
—	7¾ **Wetherby** ... arr	6 52	..	..	7 51	..	..	8 26	..	..	..	..	..	1243	..	..	..	..	..	4 53	..	..	..	..	..	..	..	..	..	..	..
—	Wetherby ... dep	..	..	..	..	..	7 58	..	..	..	..	..	..	..	12 50	2 8	..	..	..	..	..	5 11	..	..	..	..	7 15	..	..	..	..
17¾	Thorp Arch **A** ...	..	..	..	..	..	8 4	..	..	..	..	..	..	..	12 56	2 14	..	..	..	..	..	5 17	..	..	..	..	7 22	..	..	..	..
19¼	Newton Kyme ...	..	..	..	..	..	8 8	..	..	..	..	..	..	..	1 0	2 18	..	..	..	..	..	5 21	..	..	..	..	7 26	..	..	..	..
21½	Tadcaster ...	..	..	..	..	..	8 12	..	..	..	..	..	..	..	1 4	2 22	..	..	..	..	..	5 25	..	..	..	..	7 31	..	..	..	..
26	Church Fenton ... arr	..	..	..	..	..	8 19	..	..	..	..	..	..	..	1 11	2 29	..	..	..	..	..	5 32	..	..	..	..	7 38	..	..	..	..
36¾	113 YORK 116 ... arr	..	..	..	..	..	8 57	..	..	..	..	..	..	..	2 28	3 39	..	..	..	..	..	6 8	..	..	..	..	10 9	..	..	..	..
36½	104 SELBY ... "	..	..	..	..	..	8 46	..	..	..	..	..	..	..	..	..	..	..	..	..	..	6 11	..	..	..	..	..	..	..	..	..
67	104 HULL ... "	..	..	..	..	..	9 48	..	..	..	..	..	..	..	..	..	..	..	..	..	..	7 51	..	..	..	..	..	..	..	..	..

A Station for Boston Spa (1¼ miles) **S** or S Saturday only **X** One class only

For **LOCAL TRAINS** between Cross Gates and Leeds, see Table 115

For **OTHER TRAINS** between Church Fenton and Leeds, see Tables 104, 116—Harrogate and Leeds, Table 121

Above left:
Harrogate was a considerable rail centre in the 1950s, with lines radiating out towards Leeds, Church Fenton, York, Boroughbridge, Ripon and Pateley Bridge and it possessed a sizeable station to handle these various services. Gradually, however, these services were to be withdrawn; the first to succumb being that to Pilmoor, via Knaresborough and Boroughbridge, which closed in 1950. As services disappeared so the facilities at Harrogate were reduced and the station was remodelled in the 1960s. In happier times, 'Hunt' class 4-4-0 No 62765 *Goathland* arrives with a service from York. *Real Photographs*

Above:
Jubilee' No 45562 *Alberta* hauls the royal train as an ECS working from Ripon to York on 30 May 1967. The train is seen crossing the River Nidd between Bilton Road signalbox and Nidd Bridge. Based at Holbeck, *Alberta* was the oldest (being built in August 1934) of a trio of the class to survive over the summer of 1967. In the company of Nos 45593 *Kolhapur* and 45697 *Achilles*, the three locomotives were to act as a magnet for enthusiasts during that final summer. *Alberta* was the last to be withdrawn, finally succumbing in November of that year. Of the trio, only *Kolhapur* was to survive into preservation. *C. E. Weston*

Above:
On 24 April 1962 there was a stranger on the Neville Hill-Church Fenton pick-up goods in the guise of 'Jubilee' No 45708 *Resolution*. It is seen here at Bardsey on the Wetherby-Cross Gates line heading tender-first back towards Leeds. The line from Wetherby to Cross Gates was to close completely on 27 April 1964; passenger services having been withdrawn three months earlier. *J. M. Rayner*

Below:
One of the region's 'forgotten' lines was that which linked Arthington (on the Leeds-Harrogate line) with Burley in Wharfedale (on the Leeds-Ilkley route). Serving Pool and Otley, it was a useful link between the North Eastern and Midland railways avoiding Leeds. 'B16' No 61478, one of the Raven-designed 4-6-0s of 1920, takes the north-west curve at Arthington *en route* for Skipton with a special from Wetherby racecourse. It was over this line that the North Eastern Railway operated a through Harrogate-Bradford (Forster Square) service exercising running powers over MR metals into the city. This service was to survive until 1957; the last passenger services ran over the line in 1965 and it was closed completely on 5 July that year.
J. Pawley

Above:
The line from Leeds, via Arthington, to Harrogate formed part of the North Eastern Railway's main line through Ripon to Northallerton. Until the section north of Harrogate closed in 1967, the route saw a great variety of express passenger and freight services. In 1950, 'Hunt' class 4-4-0 No 62772 *The Sinnington* is seen near Arthington with a Harrogate-Leeds express. *H. Weston*

Below:
Also on the Leeds-Harrogate line, at Bramhope, 'B1' No 61069, at this time allocated to Neville Hill, heads a Leeds-Harrogate local service on 9 August 1949. The Thompson-designed 'B1s' were to see service in the West Riding almost until the end of steam operation in the area in 1967. *H. Weston*

60025

Above left:
Scholes was the first station north of Cross Gates on the ex-North Eastern line to Wetherby. On 31 July 1957 'B16' 4-6-0 No 61432 and 'Austerity' 2-8-0 No 90026 double-head a northbound freight through the station. *M. Mitchell*

Below left:
The classic lines of Gresley's immortal 'A4' Pacifics were seen regularly in the West Riding predominantly running over the East Coast main line north from Doncaster through Selby to York or to Leeds and beyond. On 22 May 1959 King's Cross-allocated No 60025 *Falcon* was the motive power for the southbound 'Talisman', which is seen south of Selby. *Brian Morrison*

Above:
'Crab' No 42704, then allocated to Newton Heath, crosses Arthington Viaduct on 3 August 1955 with a Bradford Forster Square-Saltburn excursion. This was the first working of an LMR locomotive throughout and the train also included, unusually, a WR coach. The train would have been routed over the Otley & Ilkley Joint line from Guiseley to Otley, before joining the ex-NER route at Arthington.
J. W. C. Halliday

Right:
The ex-NER line to Wetherby diverged from the main Leeds-York main line at Cross Gates. Here, as 'A3' Pacific No 60086 *Gainsborough* approaches the station with the 9.55am Newcastle-Liverpool (Lime Street) service on 30 July 1960, the Wetherby line can be seen heading away to the north. The Wetherby line lost its passenger services on 6 January 1964 and its freight services three months later, on 27 April. More recently, however, the erstwhile West Yorkshire Metropolitan County Council viewed the line as having a potential in the long term for reopening in part. *J. M. Rayner*

Above:
'V2' No 60885 emerges from the short tunnel at Weeton, just south of Harrogate on the line towards Leeds, with the Saturdays Only 9.43am Darlington-Manchester service on 20 July 1963. *M. Mitchell*

Above right:
Arthington was the point where the ex-NER branch to Otley diverged from the Leeds-Harrogate main line. Here 'B16/2' No 61435 is seen heading north with an RCTS special. The station at Arthington closed on 22 March 1965, at the same time as passenger services were withdrawn on the branch to Otley and Guiseley. *M. York*

Below right:
Newton Kyme was situated on the ex-NER line from Harrogate, via Wetherby and Tadcaster, to Church Fenton. 'B16' No 61447 is pictured picking up at the station with an excursion to Bridlington in June 1959. Despite serving the towns of Wetherby and Tadcaster, both famous for their racecourses and the latter for its breweries, the line was to close to passenger services on 6 January 1964. Freight services over the Wetherby-Tadcaster section were withdrawn on 4 April 1966 and the remaining section, from Tadcaster to Church Fenton on 30 November 1966.
P. Sunderland

RCTS
61435

Above:
Ex-LMS '4F' No 44070 speeds towards the goods-only station at Stutton, on the Tadcaster-Church Fenton line with a service from Tadcaster to Sheffield in May 1959.
Peter Sunderland

Below:
On 24 June 1963 Raven-designed 'Q6' 0-8-0 No 63417 is seen climbing away from Bardsey, between Wetherby and Cross Gates, with the Church Fenton-Neville Hill pick-up goods. *J. M. Rayner*

Above:
'J39' No 64863 is seen wrong line at Wetherby old station having just run round its stock for a race-goers' special. The old station, which can be seen in the background, was situated on the route towards Tadcaster; it was replaced by a station at the junction of the lines to Harrogate and Tadcaster when the direct west-south link was opened in 1905. *Kenneth Field*

Below:
'Hunt' class 4-4-0 No 62772 *The Sinnington* awaits departure from Harrogate with a through train to Knaresborough. This was one of a total of 75 'D49s' constructed to a design of Sir Nigel Gresley from 1927. Harrogate station, following the loss of many of its services, was significantly remodelled during the 1960s. The line through Knaresborough to York is one of the town's two surviving railway links. *Kenneth Field*

Leeds

The place of Leeds in the railway history of Britain is assured as it was close to the town that the first railway built under an Act of Parliament — the Middleton — was constructed. It received its parliamentary approval on 9 June 1758. It was to be a further 75 years before Leeds was to be added to the growing list of towns provided with a main line link when the Leeds & Selby Railway opened in 1834. This line has always been regarded as the first main line in the county. The new railway was provided with a station at Marsh Lane, although this terminus was to close in 1869 when Leeds (New) station was opened. (This station was combined with Leeds Wellington to form Leeds City in 1938 and rebuilt during the 1960s.)

From these beginnings Leeds was to acquire an impressive network of railway routes radiating to all points of the compass. These lines included on 1 July 1840 the opening of the North Midland's line from Hunslet Lane southwards to Rotherham (later part of the Midland main line); the Leeds & Bradford Railway line through the Aire Valley in 1846; the London & North Western towards Dewsbury from 1848; the line through Headingley and Horsforth towards Harrogate (later the main line through Ripon to Northallerton) in 1849; and the Great Northern.

After a period of dispute, Leeds ended up with three city centre stations — Central (Great Northern and L&YR), Wellington (Midland) and New (LNWR and NER). This was a situation that persisted until the combining on New and Wellington in the late 1930s. It was not until 1967, however, that Central was to close finally with its services diverted into the rebuilt Leeds City station. There was an equally great provision of locomotive sheds: the NER stock was shedded at Neville Hill (to the east of the city) — closed to steam in June 1966; Midland locomotives at Holbeck — closed 1967; LNWR at Farnley Junction — closed 1966; and, Great Northern at Copley Hill — closed 1964. At the Grouping in 1923 Holbeck and Farnley

Below:
In June 1950, two years after Nationalisation, nothing seems to have changed for ex-LNER 'B4' No 1482 *Immingham* at Ardsley shed. Destined for imminent withdrawal, by this time the locomotive was the last of the class in service. A total of 10 'B4s' had been built to a design of Robinson in 1906. Ardsley, situated on the Wakefield-Leeds main line, was one of the most important ex-GN sheds in the West Riding, with an allocation of 88 locomotives in 1950. Originally an Eastern Region shed, it was later transferred to the North Eastern Region. It was to close in 1965. *Real Photographs*

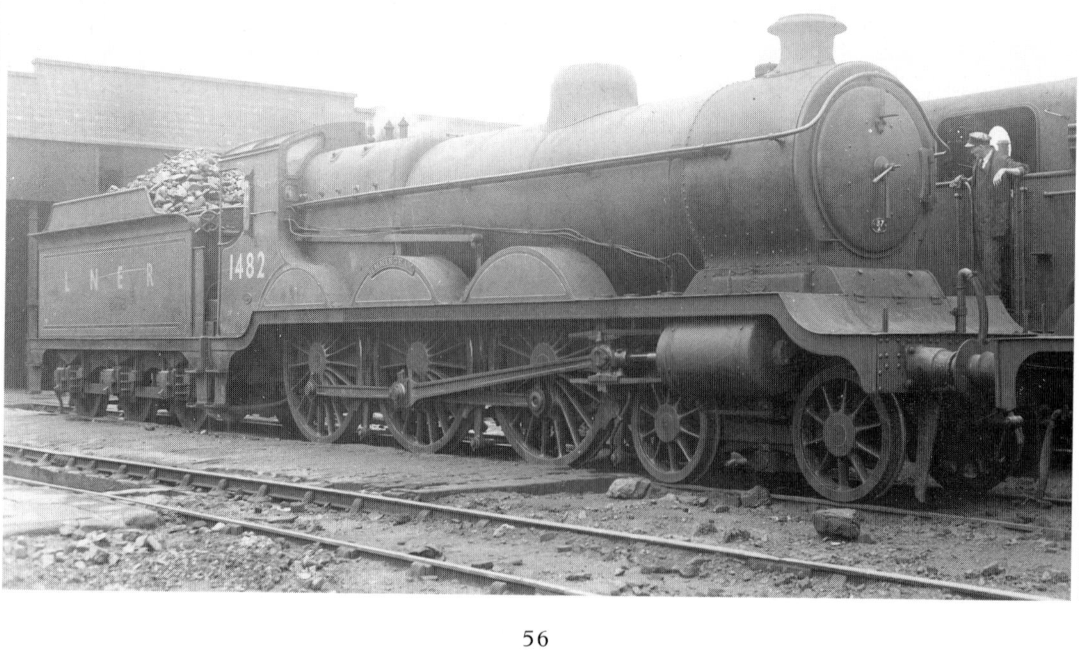

Junction passed to the LMS, the remaining two to the LNER. Ultimately, under BR, all the sheds passed to the North Eastern Region and this led increasingly to non-typical locomotive allocations — particularly after the closure of Copley Hill when several ex-LNER Pacifics were transferred to Holbeck.

As befitted a city of Leeds' importance, it was served by a number of prestige services — such as the 'Thames-Clyde' and the 'White Rose' — which brought express passenger locomotives to the city. In later years, however, Leeds became best-known amongst railway enthusiasts as the home of 'Jubilees' which survived the withdrawal of the remainder of the class by several months and which ran through the summer of 1967. The exploits of the Holbeck 'Jubilees' — such as *Alberta* and *Kolhapur* — were well-recorded and perhaps marked the final swansong of steam operation in the county.

Although there were a number of closures affecting Leeds — in particular the withdrawal of services over the LNWR's 'New Line' towards Huddersfield — Leeds itself emerged relatively unscathed from the decimation of the railway network in the years before 1968. Later, prior to the inauguration of main line electrification, Leeds resounded to the sound of steam once again as it was used as the departure point for regular steam specials over the Settle & Carlisle and Harrogate/York lines. Although these have now ceased, it is still possible to see and ride behind steam in the city — courtesy of the pioneering, and now preserved, Middleton Railway.

Above:
Holbeck in Leeds was the Midland Railway's main shed serving Leeds. Situated on the main line from Whitehall Junction towards Stourton, the shed was home to many top-link passenger locomotives, including in 1959 almost 20 'Jubilees' and five 'Royal Scots'. By that date, however, '2P' No 40323, seen at Holbeck on 26 August 1955, had been withdrawn. Built in 1914 at Derby, No 40323 had had an eventful career. Constructed originally for the Somerset & Dorset Joint (as that line's No 71 and renumbered to No 40 in 1928), it became LMS No 323 when the LMS absorbed the ex-S&D locomotives in 1930. It was to be one of the last two ex-S&D 4-4-0s to survive in service, being withdrawn in September 1956. *Brian Morrison*

Above:
'Black 5' No 45191 heads towards Ardsley tunnel, south of Leeds, with the 3.5pm Bradford-King's Cross express on 6 August 1966. The train is passing under the bridge which carried the ex-Great Northern Beeston-Tingley-Batley line over the ex-GN main line. The Beeston-Batley line had closed on 6 July 1953. *M. Mitchell*

Above right:
By 13 April 1966, the date of this photograph, Leeds (Central) station had barely a year to survive before its closure with its services diverted into the rebuilt Leeds (City). 'Jubilee' No 45697, formerly named *Achilles*, is seen awaiting the right away with a local service for Doncaster. Ironically, *Achilles* was to become one of the final three 'Jubilees' to remain in service and was to outlive Central station by several months the following year. *Dr L. A. Nixon*

Below right:
'Jubilee' No 45652 *Hawke* heads past the Midland box at Altofts Junction with the 11.18am Bradford (Forster Square)-London (St Pancras) express on 27 July 1958. The ex-North Eastern line towards York heads off to the right.
A. Robey

B6
45697

ALTOFTS JCT
45652

Above:
Considered by many to be amongst the most unattractive of steam locomotive designs, the Ivatt '4MT' 2-6-0s were introduced in 1947. A total of 162 were built, the majority entering service after Nationalisation. A number, such as No 43115 seen here at Holbeck with the shed's breakdown train (including a steam crane) on 27 August 1955, were based at sheds in the West Riding. The early locomotives of the class had been built with double chimneys; later examples (from No 43050 onwards) were constructed with single chimneys, and the earlier-built models were also to receive single chimneys eventually. *Brian Morrison*

Above right:
By the early 1950s, representatives of many of the pre-Grouping classes were beginning to disappear. Amongst the casualties at this time were the last surviving examples of locomotives inherited from the Hull & Barnsley Railway. A total of 138 H&BR locomotives passed (via the NER) to the LNER in 1923. Of these, only 12 survived until Nationalisation and only one remained in service in 1955. This sole survivor was 'N13' No 69114, which is seen in Neville Hill shed, Leeds, on 26 August 1955 just before withdrawal. Originally designed by Stirling and entering service in 1913, No 69114 was, like all other ex-H&BR locomotives, to pass to the scrapman. *Brian Morrison*

Below right:
Class 5 No 45232 pilots 'Jubilee' No 45735 *Atlas* along the Leeds-Morley-Huddersfield line near Farnley Junction, on the outskirts of Leeds, with the afternoon ECS train on 16 August 1962. The overbridge visible in the background carried the up line of the LNWR's Leeds-Huddersfield 'New Line'. *M. Mitchell*

Leeds Neville Hill (50B)
Allocation as at 1959

Class 2	41247
Class A3	60036 *Colombo*, 60074 *Harvester*, 60081 *Shotover*, 60084 *Trigo*
Class B1	61016 *Inyala*, 61035 *Pronghorn*, 61038 *Blacktail*, 61062, 61216, 61218, 61237 *Geoffrey H. Kitson*, 61240 *Harry Hinchcliffe*, 61257, 61259
Class B16	61411, 61412, 61414, 61415, 61425, 61427, 61428, 61429, 61431, 61432, 61442, 61446, 61447, 61470, 61471
Class J39	64725, 64730, 64758, 64835, 64850, 64863, 64870, 64920, 64922, 64933, 64934, 64935, 64943
Class 3	77004, 77013
Class 4	80116, 80117, 80118, 80119, 80120
Class WD	90026, 90045, 90467, 90663...

69114

WARDS SIDING
45232
40

Above:
A Newcastle-Liverpool express, double-headed by 'Jubilee' No 45723 *Fearless* and 'Patriot' No 45527 *Southport*, coasts downhill through the heart of the West Riding's Heavy Woollen District between Batley and Dewsbury (Wellington Road). Immediately to the left of the train and just out of sight at a lower level is the ex-GN Bradford-Dewsbury (Central)-Wakefield Westgate route. *A. M. Ross*

Below:
'Jubilee' No 45593 *Kolhapur* and 'Black 5' No 45392 await departure from the rebuilt Leeds City station on Saturday 22 July 1967. Both trains had been delayed on this occasion by the failure of an earlier DMU. No 45593 sports the diagonal yellow stripe on the cabside indicating that the locomotive was precluded from operating south of Crewe over the electrified lines. *Michael Turner*

Above:
'Jubilee' No 45581 *Bihar* and *Orissa* and 'Britannia' No 70015 *Apollo* await the right away from platform No 11 at Leeds City with the 10.42pm mail train to Shrewsbury on 9 July 1965. Delivered in June 1951 No 70015 was originally a Western Region locomotive, although had been loaned to the London Midland Region when new. As with all the 'Britannias' the locomotive was to end its days allocated to the LMR and, at this time, had only just been reallocated to Stockport from Crewe North. *Apollo* was withdrawn from Kingmoor in August 1967. *G. M. S. Carter*

Right:
On 3 March 1967 the last steam-hauled 8.1pm service from Leeds City to Skipton was hauled by one of Holbeck's famous 'Jubilees' — No 45593 *Kolhapur.* It is seen here awaiting departure. *J. B. Mounsey*

E 9340
42184

Stourton (55B)
Allocation as at 1959

Class 4	43014, 43038, 43044
Class 3F	43456, 43681, 43737
Class 4F	43871, 43931, 43968, 43987, 44028, 44044, 44094, 44153, 44207, 44238, 44335, 44368, 44467, 44570, 44584, 44586
Class 8F	48055, 48076, 48084, 48126, 48160, 48276, 48311, 48352, 48358, 48622, 48641, 48652, 48703, 48721

Left:
Fairburn 2-6-4T No 42184 shunts empty coaching stock at the east end of Leeds City station on 17 August 1965. In the background a DMU awaits departure and prominent on the skyline is the roof of the city's famous Corn Exchange — a building regularly used to house model railway exhibitions.
J. H. Cooper-Smith

Above:
A panoramic view of the western approaches to Leeds. On the left can be seen Holbeck shed with an impressive array of steam locomotives on shed, along with early indications of the new order (a diesel shunter and Type 2 diesel-electric); above the train and signalbox can be seen the ex-LNWR viaduct which carried the Leeds 'New' line into the city. Following the closure of the 'New' in the 1960s the western end of the route at this point was modified to link with the ex-GNR main line towards Wakefield, thus allowing an alternative exit from Leeds for Wakefield-bound trains. The link was finally severed with the electrification of the East Coast main line.
Ian Allan Library

Left:
On 6 August 1956 Class N1 0-6-2T No 69430 is seen near Beeston Junction with the 2.44pm Leeds Central-Castleford train.
B. K. B Green

Centre left:
Ex-LNER 'J50/4' No 68988, built at Gorton in 1939, is pictured shunting at Holbeck (High Level) on 29 April 1949. At this date, although the locomotive has gained a smokebox numberplate and 'British Railways' legend, the coaching stock, albeit renumbered, remains in LNER livery.
H. C. Casserley

Below left:
With the form of the new roof at Leeds City taking shape above it and with evidence of the rebuilding work on the platforms, 'Jubilee' No 45597 *Barbados* is caught shunting parcels vans on 12 February 1964. Work started on the rebuilding of Leeds City station in the early 1960s with completion in early 1967. Upon completion the ex-GNR Central station was closed and services diverted into the rebuilt City.
B. J. Ashworth

Above right:
On 8 August 1964 'Black 5' No 45411 is pictured emerging from the 1 mile 1,609yd Morley Tunnel with the Saturdays Only 10am service from Sunderland to Manchester. *M. Mitchell*

Below right:
A powerful combination of 'B1' No 61337 and 'Britannia' No 70010 *Owen Glendower* head an afternoon York-Manchester ECS near Farnley Junction on the ex-LNWR main line on 16 July 1965. The 'Britannia' had only been transferred to Carlisle Kingmoor from Crewe South the previous month. The locomotives have just passed under the bridge carrying the ex-LNWR 'New Line' towards Heckmondwike. *M. Mitchell*

61337

Above:
'N1' No 69432 is photographed leaving platform No 2 at Leeds Central station with the 4.35pm service to Bradford Exchange on 2 June 1954. Leeds Central was the ex-GNR terminus in the city; it retained services until they were transferred to the rebuilt Leeds City station early in 1967. Subsequently much of the station site has been redeveloped, although it is still possible to see traces of the railway's presence. *R. Jackson*

Below:
'Jubilee' No 45695 *Minotaur* pilots sister locomotive No 45645 *Collingwood* out of an unrebuilt Leeds City station with a Hull-Liverpool express. At a lower level can be seen coaching stock stabled in the ex-Midland Wellington station, whilst dominating the background is the dramatic skyline of the ex-LMS Queens Hotel. Designed by W. Curtis Green (who also designed the Dorchester Hotel in London) and by the LMS's own architect, W. H. Hamlyn, the rebuilt hotel opened in 1937. The hotel remained under the ownership of British Transport Hotels until privatised in the early 1980s. *J. R. Carter*

Farnley Junction (55C)
Allocation as at 1959

Class 2P	40584
Class 2	41254, 41255, 41256, 41258, 41259
Class 6P5F	42713, 42766, 42789, 42865, 42866
Class 5	44896, 45063, 45075, 45079, 45080, 45204, 45211
'Jubilee'	45581 *Bihar & Orissa*, 45646 *Napier*, 45695 *Minotaur*, 45708 *Resolution*
Class 3F	47568, 47569, 47570
Class WD	90127, 90254, 90308, 90318, 90322, 90334, 90336, 90351, 90395, 90407, 90562, 90588, 90591, 90645, 90649, 90650, 90664, 90666, 90684, 90699, 90726, 90728

Above:
On 10 August 1960 'J50' 0-6-0T No 68900 was photographed shunting at Ardsley, south of Leeds, on the ex-GNR main line to Doncaster. The lines on the extreme left formed the ex-GNR route to Bradford via Morley, which closed to passenger services on 4 July 1966 and to freight on 5 May 1969. Today the scene is radically different, with the 25kV ac electrified route to Leeds being bisected by the trans-Pennine M62 motorway.
M. Mitchell

Calderdale

It was through the Calder Valley that railways first breached the barrier of the Pennines. The Manchester & Leeds Railway (later the Lancashire & Yorkshire Railway) opened between Manchester and Littleborough, on the west, in 1839 and from Normanton to Hebden Bridge, on the east, in the following year. The stretch through the long Summit Tunnel was opened in March 1841. The link from Greetland into Halifax was opened in July 1844 to a station at Shaw Syke, which sufficed as the town's station until the completion of the line through to Low Moor in 1850, when the new station was opened. The line from Milner Royd Junction to Halifax opened two years later.

Further west, the line from Todmorden, through Copy Pit, opened in 1849 whilst the branches to Rishworth and Stainland followed in 1878 and 1875 respectively. To the east of Sowerby Bridge, the L&YR main line towards Wakefield was to form a link with numerous other lines. From Mirfield a line, through the Spen Valley to Low Moor, opened in 1848. The same year was to witness the opening of the LNWR main line through Dewsbury to Leeds; the section from Heaton Lodge to Huddersfield had opened the previous year. The Midland Railway's freight-only branch towards Huddersfield also met the L&YR main line at Mirfield; the MR, without independent access to this point, exercised running powers over the L&YR main line from Dewsbury westwards. The Midland, with its ambitious scheme, to build a main line through the Spen Valley was to become the final pre-Grouping player in this part of the West Riding, but its grandiose plans petered out at Dewsbury. The MR's line was opened in 1905, five years after the completion of the LNWR's 'New' line to Leeds.

The L&YR, LNWR and MR were all eventually merged into the LMS in 1923. The process of rationalisation started relatively early; two lines — those to Stainland and Rishworth — lost their passenger services in the 1920s, while the Pickle Bridge line was not to last long under BR control — it lost its passenger services in June 1948. The rest of the network was, however, to survive into the Beeching years when closure came rapidly for the bulk of the lines: the ex-MR line from Royston to Thornhill in 1960; the Mirfield-Low Moor line in April 1965 (it remained open for freight until the early 1980s and now forms part of the proposed West Yorkshire Transport Museum project); Thornhill-Heckmondwike in June 1965; the Leeds 'New' line in August 1965; and, the Copy Pit line in November 1965 (the route was subsequently reopened). Even the ex-L&YR main line east of Sowerby Bridge was not immune; it was closed in January 1970 between Sowerby Bridge and Heaton Lodge to passenger services.

The ex-L&YR main line, with its regular trans-Pennine coal trains, was to remain one of the most important steam-hauled main lines right through until the end of steam operation on the North Eastern Region.

Sowerby Bridge (56E)
Allocation as at 1959

Class 3	40147
Class 4	42094, 42149, 42150, 42151, 42311, 42380, 42405
Class 4	43126
Class 3F	47266, 47299, 47379, 47508, 47509
Class 3F	52351, 52400, 52411, 52452
Class WD	90113, 90122, 90210, 90310, 90329, 90360, 90412, 90470

Below left:
Halifax Town was the ex-Lancashire & Yorkshire Railway station in the town. The station had been opened with the extension of the L&YR line from Halifax to Low Moor in August 1850 and replaced an older station. Known as Halifax (Old) until renamed 'Town' on 30 September 1951 the station was also to be served by Great Northern trains following the opening of the lines to Keighley and Bradford via Queensbury. With the closure of Halifax (North Bridge) station, the station was to lose its 'Town' suffix on 12 June 1961. In October 1956 '4P' 2-6-4T No 42310 awaits departure with a service for London King's Cross. Until the closure of the ex-GN routes the previous year this train would have been routed via Queensbury. *Real Photographs*

Above right:
Shortly after leaving Greetland, ex-L&YR 0-6-0 No 52400 (allocated to Sowerby Bridge) heads up the gradient towards West Vale.
Geoff Lumb

Right:
The village of West Vale was dominated by the viaduct constructed by the L&YR as part of the 1½ mile long Greetland-Stainland branch. Opened in 1875, passenger services over the line were withdrawn as early as 23 September 1929 as a result of competition from Halifax's trams. Freight services, however, were to continue for some 30 years thereafter and occasional excursions also graced the branch. The mill chimney to the left of the viaduct is of particular significance to the author, as it belonged to Onecliffe Mills, home of Waller Bros (West Vale) Ltd (a firm founded by his grandfather and great-uncle). The viaduct bisected the firm's land and the company rented the space beneath the arches for a variety of outbuildings connected with the business. *Geoff Lumb*

BRITISH RAILWAYS
STAINLAND BRANCH CLOSURE
The British Transport Commission regret that because of the loss which is being incurred the Section of Line between Greetland (exclusive) and Stainland (inclusive) will be closed on and from Monday September 14th 1959.
This course has been approved by the Yorkshire Area Transport Users' Consultative Committee and the Central Transport Consultative Committee.
The motor vehicles based on Halifax which now collect and deliver smalls freight traffic will continue to do so.
The alternative freight depot for full load traffic is Greetland.
Further information may be obtained from the District Goods Superintendent, City Station, Leeds, 1.

Above:
Normanton-based Ivatt 2-6-0 No 43114 heads through Greetland with a train for Normanton on 6 May 1959. The Stainland branch can be seen swinging away to the south in the distance. *Geoff Lumb*

Left:
A sign of the times — despite the presence of many textile mills along the route, including the huge complex of Brookroyd Mills at Stainland, it proved impossible to retain the freight service. The final closure came on 14 September 1959. Thereafter, until lifted, the northernmost part of the branch was used to store redundant wagons. *Geoff Lumb*

Above right:
Stanier 'Class 5' No 44907 crosses over the River Calder near Mirfield with a Leeds City-Manchester relief train on Whit Sunday 5 June 1965. J. *B. Mounsey*

Below right:
On 31 May 1962 Class 8F No 48123 runs over the water troughs at Luddenden Foot, in the Calder Valley, with a westbound coal train from Yorkshire across the Pennines. In the distance can be seen Halifax and the prominent Wainhouse Tower. This 253ft tower was constructed in the 1870s and was designed to serve as a chimney for the dye-works owned by J. E. Wainhouse. At this date (and indeed up until withdrawal in 1967) No 48123 was a Royston-based locomotive. *D. I. Wood*

48123

45368

Left:
With the cooling towers of Thornhill power station in the background, Class 5 4-6-0 No 45368 heads the Saturdays Only 10.32am Scarborough-Manchester Victoria service through the Calder Valley on 22 August 1964. One of the smallest coal-fired power stations in the region, Thornhill was rail-served for many years. *J. B. Mounsey*

Above right:
Ardsley-based 'K3' 2-6-0 No 61853 heads a Summer Saturday relief from Blackpool on 6 August 1960 on to the Calder Valley line at Todmorden from the Copy Pit route. Designed by Gresley and introduced in 1924, a total of 193 of the 'K3s' were built. The majority of the class survived until the early 1960s, but the last, including No 61853, were withdrawn in December 1962. *R. S. Greenwood*

Centre right:
'Jubilee' 4-6-0 No 45565 *Victoria* approaches Luddenden Foot on 23 July 1966 with the 1.25pm Blackpool North-Bradford Exchange service. Originally delivered in August 1934, this locomotive had, the previous month, been returned from Wakefield (where it had been transferred in February) to Low Moor, its home from June 1962 until withdrawal in January 1967. *Ian G. Holt*

Below right:
Blackpool-based 'Jubilee' No 45705 *Seahorse* speeds towards Mytholmroyd along the Calder Valley line on 6 July 1963 with a Saturday service from its home town to Lincoln. The train worked over the Copy Pit route, reaching the Calder Valley line at Todmorden. On the adjacent loop is a train of empty coal wagons. *Ian G. Holt*

Above:
'Black 5' No 45208 gives rear end assistance to sister loco No 44694 with the Saturdays Only 1.25pm Bridlington-Bradford Exchange service as it ascends Greetland Bank on 5 August 1967. The line from Greetland to Halifax, which was opened on 1 July 1848, was the first railway link to the latter town. In later years services declined until it became effectively freight-only. At the time of writing the track is 'mothballed', although there are hopes that the 1990s may witness a restored Halifax-Huddersfield passenger service over the line. *M. Mitchell*

Left:
On 4 August 1968, a week before the final demise of main line steam, two 'Black 5s', Nos 44871 and 44894, were provided to haul the SLS 'A' tour from Birmingham to Manchester and Wigan. The two are seen leaving Hall Royd Junction, Todmorden. No 44871 was later to achieve fame as one of the 'Black 5s' used on the 15 Guinea 'Farewell to Steam' special but, unlike the other locomotives used on that special, was not to survive into preservation.
John M. Boyes

Above right:
On 8 August 1964 'B1' 4-6-0 No 61338 heads homeward through the Calder Valley with the Saturdays Only 10.45am Blackpool-Lincoln service.
J. B. Mounsey

Below right:
With one of the region's many textile mills in the background, 'Black 5' No 45207 heads eastbound towards Brighouse on 9 May 1962 with a return working of empty mineral wagons. This section of the ex-L&YR Calder Valley main line was to lose its regular passenger services in 1970, leaving Brighouse as one of the largest towns in the West Riding without a passenger service.
D. I. Wood

EC 941

Above left:
Leaving a trail of smoke behind it, Standard Class 5 No 73158 makes its way past Thornhill with the Saturdays Only 10am Sunderland-Manchester Victoria service on 22 August 1964. *J. B. Mounsey*

Below left:
Heading south towards Huddersfield through Bradley Junction, 'Austerity' 2-8-0 No 90641 is pictured coming off the Bradley Wood Junction-Bradley curve with an 18-coach train of excursion stock. The train is seen passing the site of Bradley station, which closed on 6 March 1950. *Kenneth Field*

Above right:
In the decade prior to the outbreak of World War 1 the Midland Railway had an ambitious scheme for the construction of a cut-off route from Royston, through the Spen Valley, to Bradford where it would link up with the line to Forster Square station. The advantage for the MR was that such a route was slightly shorter than its existing route to Scotland and for Bradford the plan would have placed the city on a through main line. In the event only the section from Royston to Dewsbury was completed with a link from Middlestown Junction to the L&YR main line at Thornhill. On 28 June 1958 'Black 5' No 45279 ascends towards Middlestown Junction with a Blackpool North-Sheffield Midland service. The ex-MR lines towards Dewsbury Savile Town, which had closed on 18 December 1950, were by this time being used for the storage of condemned wagons in the summer and excursion stock in the winter.
A. M. Ross

Centre right:
The Halifax and Huddersfield through coaches to King's Cross drift through the winter conditions at Brighouse on 23 January 1965 behind Fairburn 2-6-4T No 42116.
J. B. Mounsey

Below right:
The Saturdays Only 2.42pm Manchester Victoria-Halifax slow train leaves Todmorden station on 6 August 1960 behind Farnley-based 'Crab' No 62774. In the background can be seen the Copy Pit banking engines — another 'Crab' and an 'Austerity' 2-8-0.
R. S. Greenwood

Above left:
On 4 August 1962 an unidentified 'Austerity' 2-8-0 heads eastbound with a rake of empty mineral wagons through Todmorden station. The impressive castellated building on the hillside is Dobroyd Castle, which dates to 1869 and was designed by John Gibson. *R. S. Greenwood*

Below left:
On 6 August 1960 the Saturdays Only 2.15pm Wakefield Kirkgate-Manchester Victoria service is seen passing Hall Royd Junction signalbox behind a pair of 'B1' 4-6-0s Nos 61015 *Duiker* and 61017 *Bushbuck*. The two running lines on the extreme left are those for the Copy Pit line towards Burnley. On the skyline in the distance can be seen Stoodley Pike. *R. S. Greenwood*

Above right:
On 16 July 1965 '4F' No 43968 hauls a short coal train from the Crigglestone line on to the Midland main line at Royston. The Crigglestone route, conceived as part of a through main line to Bradford, was not completed beyond Dewsbury and never fulfilled expectations. The failure of the Midland's ambitious scheme was to ensure that Bradford was never to be placed on a through main line. Freight services over the Crigglestone-Royston Junction route were finally transferred away on 4 May 1968. *M. Mitchell*

Centre right:
'Black 5' No 44896 emerges from the long Morley Tunnel on 28 August 1965 with the 9.3am Saturdays Only service from Leeds City to Llandudno. *M. Mitchell*

Below right:
On 6 August 1966 'Black 5' No 45494 heads the 9.14am Saturdays Only Llandudno-Newcastle service near Lady Anne Crossing, Batley, on the ex-London & North Western main line to Leeds. *M. Mitchell*

Wakefield

The city of Wakefield has long been one of the most important crossroads in the West Riding and, with its two stations of Kirkgate and Westgate, it was also to be an important railway centre as well. Situated on both north-south and east-west main lines, the city was to see a great variety of both passenger and freight services; the latter, given Wakefield's location in the centre of an important coal mining area, were of particular significance.

The first railway line in the district, the North Midland (later part of the Midland main line to Leeds), did not directly serve Wakefield but provided a station called 'Wakefield' some distance from the city. The first direct link came with the opening of the Manchester & Leeds Railway's line from Hebden Bridge to Goose Hill Junction on 8 October 1840; the opening of the line gave Wakefield its first station, which was later known as Kirkgate. A direct link with Goole came with the construction of the Wakefield, Pontefract & Goole Railway; by the time this line opened in 1848 both the M&L and WPG had been absorbed into the Lancashire & Yorkshire Railway.

The third of the major pre-Grouping companies to serve Wakefield was the Great Northern, which reached a temporary station (later Westgate) through the offices of the Bradford, Wakefield & Leeds Railway in 1857. It was not until a decade later, in 1866, that Wakefield was linked to Doncaster and its position on the GNR's main line from the West Riding southwards assured. The GNR during the 1850s and 1860s constructed a network of lines that served the area between Wakefield and Bradford. These lines allowed for the operation of a Wakefield-Bradford service via Ossett, Dewsbury and Batley, whilst it was normal procedure (once the Wakefield-Doncaster section was opened) for express services from London to be divided at Wakefield with one portion heading for Leeds and a second heading for Bradford over the Ardsley-Laisterdyke line.

Grouping in 1923 brought the GNR under the control of the LNER whilst both the Midland and L&YR passed to the LMS. The traditional rivalry in the city was, therefore, destined to remain until Nationalisation in 1948. However, with all the railways under a common ownership it was possible to rationalise many of the duplicate routes. In particular the ex-GNR lines between Wakefield and Bradford were to be radically pruned during the 1960s. All were closed with the exception of the main line to Leeds (and the line from Leeds to Bradford), with the result that,

Below:

Wakefield Kirkgate was the first railway station in the city and was opened by the Manchester & Leeds Railway (later L&YR) in October 1840. With the coming of the Great Northern in the 1850s, the station was, like Bradford (Exchange), to become a joint L&Y/GN operation until the opening of the GNR's Westgate station. The ex-L&YR main line through Wakefield was an important route for both passenger and freight services and Kirkgate was an essential junction with services heading west towards Lancashire, east towards Goole, south towards Barnsley and north towards Leeds. In May 1956 Fowler 2-6-4T No 42324 waits under the station's overall roof with a Sowerby Bridge-Goole train. *Real Photographs*

where through Bradford portions remained, these were now routed via Copley in Leeds. Passenger services, however, continue to serve both Westgate and Kirkgate; the former, with the onset of the new electrified services has had the benefit of considerable modernisation; the latter, very much the 'Cinderella' station in Wakefield, looks much more careworn.

Wakefield shed, one of the biggest in the area had an allocation in 1950 of some 122 locomotives; of these no less than half were ex-War Department 'Austerity' 2-8-0s and the majority of the remainder were other freight classes. The dominance of coal traffic on the local railway scene cannot be overstated; there were numerous pits in the district and the throughput of empty and loaded coal wagons was enormous. Whilst many of the collieries served by rail in the district were to outlive the age of steam on the railways, the number of collieries in the area today is but a handful.

Above:
The other station in Wakefield was Westgate which opened originally in 1857. The first station on the site was converted from a private house, but this was later replaced by a grand structure in the Italianate style with prominent clocktower. Bradford (Hammerton Street)-allocated 'N1' 0-6-2T No 69464 is caught with, appropriately, the Bradford portion of a West Riding-King's Cross express in April 1950. At this time, and until the closure of the line, the majority of Bradford-London services were run over the ex-GN line from Laisterdyke via Drighlington. (This scene has changed out of all recognition with the rebuilding of the station and the electrification of the East Coast main line.) *Real Photographs*

Right:
Although only a relatively small place — and perhaps more famous for its castle than for its railways — Pontefract was graced by no less than three stations. Two were on the Wakefield-Goole line (which was the first to serve the town, opening on 1 April 1848) and the third was on the Rotherham-York line. In August 1949 an ex-L&YR 2-4-2T, still retaining its LMS number is seen at Pontefract (Tanshelf) with a Wakefield-Knottingley train. Tanshelf station was to close on 2 January 1967 when Leeds-Goole services were diverted to run (with a reversal) via Castleford. *Real Photographs*

Above:
'A4' Pacific No 60022 *Mallard* eases round the curve from Ferrybridge to Knottingley with a diverted Newcastle-King's Cross express. From this point the train would head south-eastwards over the Knottingley-Askern line before rejoining the East Coast main line at Askern Junction.
Kenneth Field

Below:
The ex-WD 2-8-0s were regular performers in the West Riding during the last years of steam with many allocated to the region's sheds. No 90175 is caught passing Royston Junction, near Wakefield, with a down freight from the Midland main line on 21 August 1965. Straddling the rear of the train can be seen the piers of the partially demolished bridge that carried the ex-Great Central line from Nostell, via Staincross, to Wharncliffe Woodmoor, which had closed on 31 July 1961. *J. S. Hancock*

Above:
On 22 May 1959 'Black 5' No 44981 hauls the Newcastle-Birmingham express past Pontefract Baghill over the Swinton & Knottingley Joint line. This line, originally owned by the Midland and North Eastern railways, was (and remains) an important link between the Sheffield area and York. *Brian Morrison*

Below:
'K1' No 62062 restarts a train of empty coal hoppers for the Sheffield line from Burton Salmon, just north of Pontefract, on 1 February 1964. The up platform of the station, which closed on 14 September 1959, occupied the area on the left of the photograph. The signals are of the North Eastern pattern with slotted posts. *J. S. Hancock*

Wakefield (56A)
Allocation as at 1959

Class 3	40117, 40139, 40155, 40169
Class 2	41264
Class 6P5F	42861, 42862, 42863
Class 4F	44019
Class 2	46413, 46435, 46438
Class 3F	47271, 47463, 47510, 47538, 47567, 47571, 47572, 47573, 47580, 47582
Class 2F	52044
Class 3F	52133, 52355
Class B1	61015 *Duiker*, 61017 *Bushbuck*, 61131, 61268, 61296, 61385
Class O4	63588, 63857, 63864, 63920
Class J50	68904, 68910, 68939
Class WD	90016, 90047, 90056, 90061, 90076, 90089, 90100, 90112, 90116, 90124, 90321, 90326, 90339, 90341, 90342, 90348, 90353, 90361, 90363, 90370, 90379, 90380, 90382, 90385, 90396, 90404, 90414, 90415, 90417, 90429, 90497, 90581, 90604, 90607, 90615, 90620, 90625, 90631, 90633, 90635, 90639, 90644, 90651, 90654, 90656, 96679, 90692, 90710, 90719

Above:
With numerous collieries, particularly around Wakefield and Barnsley, coal was a staple commodity for shipment by rail in the West Riding. Many lines and sheds survived solely for this traffic. 'Austerity' 2-8-0 No 90427 heads a coal train past Wakefield MPD on 10 December 1966. Although this particular locomotive was not allocated to Wakefield, many others of the type were — a total of 84 in 1965. Wakefield was to be one of the last West Riding sheds with an allocation of steam, being finally closed in 1967 with the end of steam on North Eastern Region.
K. P. Lawrence

Above:
Class 2MT 2-6-0 No 46493 pulls out of Pontefract Monkhill station with the Saturdays Only 1pm Knottingley-Leeds train on 4 May 1957. Alongside, Class 8F No 48622 can be seen with a coal train from Whitwood Sidings. *P. Cookson*

Below:
'Austerity' 2-8-0 No 90076, then allocated to Wakefield, was unusual motive power when used to haul the LCGB 'Crab Commemorative' railtour on 8 October 1966. The train is seen at Goole. No 90076 was to be transferred to Normanton in July 1967 and then to West Hartlepool the following month. It was withdrawn from the latter shed during September 1967. *Ian G. Holt*

Above:
On 12 July 1955 Stanier 2-6-4T No 42553, appropriately allocated to Goole, hauls the 11.49am Wakefield Kirkgate-Goole service near Featherstone. This line was to lose its passenger service on 2 January 1967 although it has subsequently been restored. *C. W. Bendall*

Below:
'A1' Pacific No 60122 *Curlew* climbs out of Wakefield Westgate with a King's Cross-Leeds Central express service. The lines on the right form the ex-Great Northern route towards Dewsbury and Bradford via Alverthorpe and Ossett. *Kenneth Field*

Ardsley (56B)
Allocation as at 1959

Class 4	43075, 43101
Class 3F	47443, 47589, 47632, 47640
Class V2	60861, 60884, 60916
Class B1	61013 *Topi*, 61110, 61123, 61295, 61297, 61310
Class O4	63570, 63584, 63605, 63633, 63724, 63823, 63885
Class J6	64182, 64208, 64222, 64268
Class J39	64705, 64720, 64732, 64749, 64754, 64757, 64760, 64806, 64811, 64820, 64825, 64831, 64833, 64836, 64837, 64839, 64840, 64879, 64918, 64969, 64979
Class J52	68824, 68834, 68869, 68875
Class J50	68890, 68900, 68901, 68902, 68914, 68915, 68916, 68935, 68937, 68938, 68947

Above:
'B1' No 61173 departs eastwards from Wakefield Kirkgate on the line to Normanton with a parcels service on 30 December 1966. The leading coach is an ex-LMS wooden-framed bogie brake, No M30973, one of a batch built at Wolverton in 1938. A number of sister coaches from this batch were to survive until the early 1980s.
J. H. Cooper-Smith

Left:
On 31 December 1966 'Austerity' 2-8-0 No 90016, which had been transferred to Goole from Hull Dairycoates that month, nears Wakefield with a coal train from the Goole direction. Visible in the background is the ex-Midland main line from Rotherham to Leeds. *J. H. Cooper-Smith*

Table 90 WAKEFIELD, DEWSBURY, BATLEY, ARDSLEY, and BRADFORD (Exchange). L·N·E·R Table 90

Week Days

Miles		a.m	a.m	a.m	a.m		a.m	a.m	a.m		a.m	a.m S		a.m S		p.m	a.m	p.m	p.m C		a.m S	a.m E	a.m S	p.m E	p.m		p.m E	p.m E	p.m	p.m S
	89 London King's C. dep	..	10K40	10K40	..	..	..	..	..	..	4 25	..	..	..	..	..	8R45	..	..		10 5	10R10	10R10	..	..	..	..	..	..	1235
	Wakefield (Kirkgate) dep	..	..	5 51	7 5	..	..	7S47	8 27	..	..	..	..	..	..	..	..	1255	..	Through Train from Scarborough (Londesborough Road), dep. 11 40 a.m. (Tables 109 and 87)	1 47	1 47	..	..	2 50	..	3 18	..	4 [illegible]	4 8
¾	" (Westgate) "	..	5 55	6 5	7 10	..	7 35	8 11	8 34	..	9 12	..	..	11 52	..	1210	1241	1 15	..		2 10	2 26	2 36	..	2 55	..	3 24	3 53	4 14	4 28
2½	Alverthorpe	..	5 59	..	Arr. Ardsley 7 20 a.m.	..	7 39	Arr. Ardsley 8 21 a.m.	8 38	..	..	..	..	11 56	..	1214	TC from King's Cross. Via Ardsley	1 19	..		TC from King's Cross. Via Ardsley	TC from King's Cross. Via Ardsley	TC from King's Cross. Via Ardsley	..	2 59	..	..	Arr. Ardsley 4 6 p.m	4 18	TC from King's Cross. Via Ardsley
4¼	Ossett	..	6 7	..		..	7 46		8 46	..	9 20	..	..	12 3	..	1221		1 26	..					..	3 6	..	..		4 24	
6¼	Earlsheaton	..	6 12	..		..	7 50		8 50	..	9 24	..	..	12 7	..	1225		1 30	..					..	3 10	..	..		4 30	
7¼	Dewsbury	..	6 16	..		..	7P56		8 53	..	9 27	..	..	12 11	..	1228		[illegible]	..					..	3 13	..	..		4 33	
7¾	Batley Carr	..	..	..		..	7 58		8 55	..	..	..	..	12 14	..	1230		1 35	..					..	..	..	..		4 35	
8½	Batley	..	6 22	..		..	8 2		8 58	..	9 31	..	..	12 18	..	1233		1 38	..					..	3 17	..	..		4 38	
9¼	Upper Batley [stall	..	6 26	..		..	8 6		9 2	..	..	..	..	..	..	1237		1 42	..					..	3 21	..	..		4 42	
10½	Howden Clough, for Bir-	..	6 30	..		..	8 10		9 6	..	..	..	..	..	..	1241		1 46	..					..	3 25	..	..		4 50	
3¼	Lofthouse A	..	..	6†13	7 16	..	..	8 17	..	..	..	..	..	..	..	..		..	..		..	..	..	..	..	..	3 30	4 [illegible]	..	
5¾	Ardsley	5 35	..	6 20	7 35	..	..	8 47	..	..	..	1127	..	..	..	..		..	1 47		..	..	..	3 0	..	..	3 36	4 15	..	
6¾	Tingley	5 40	..	6P30	7 39	..	..	8 51	..	..	..	1131	..	..	..	..		..	..		..	..	..	3 4	..	..	3 40	4 19	..	
8	Morley	5 45	..	6 36	7 43	..	..	8 55	..	..	..	1135	..	..	..	..	1256	..	1 54		2 26	2 41	2 51	3 8	..	..	3 44	4 23	..	4 43
9½	Gildersome	5 49	..	6 42	7 47	..	..	8 59	..	..	..	1139	..	..	..	..	..	..	..		..	..	..	3 12	..	..	3 48	4 27	..	..
12	Drighlington B	5 52	6 35	6 47	7 50	..	8 16	9 2	9 12	..	..	1142	..	12 30	..	1247	..	1 52	..		..	..	..	3 15	3 31	..	3 51	4 30	4 56	..
13¾	Birkenshaw and Tong	..	..	6 51	..	..	8 20	..	9 16	..	..	..	..	12 34	..	1251	..	1 56	..		..	..	..	..	3 35	..	..	..	5 0	..
15¼	Dudley Hill	..	..	6 55	..	..	8 24	..	9 20	..	..	..	..	12 38	..	1255	..	2 0	..		..	..	..	..	3 39	..	..	..	5 5	..
16¾	Laisterdyke	..	..	7 0	..	..	8 29	..	9 25	..	..	..	..	12 43	..	1 0	..	2 5	↓		..	..	..	..	3 44	..	..	..	5 10	..
18¼	St. Dunstan's arr	..	..	7 3	..	..	8 32	..	9Z30	..	..	..	..	12 46	..	1 3	..	2 8	..		..	..	..	..	3 47	..	..	..	5 13	..
18¾	Bradford (Exchange) "	..	..	7 6	..	..	8 35	..	9 30	..	9 54	..	..	12 49	..	1 6	1 15	2 11	2 15		2 47	3 0	3 10	..	3 50	..	..	..	5 16	5 2

Week Days—*continued* / **Sundays**

	p.m C		p.m D		p.m	p.m	p.m S	p.m E	p.m E	p.m S	p.m V	p.m S	p.m H	p.m K	p.m	p.m	p.m	p.m F	p.m L		p.m F	p.m	Sundays a.m	a.m	a.m		p.m	p.m		p.m		p.m	p.m
89 London (King's C.) dep	..		..		1R10	1R10	1 25	1R25	..	1R30	..	1R45	..	..	..	4R 0	..	6 5	6R 5	TC from King's Cross. Via Ardsley	6R10	..	..	10R[illegible]	10R0	..	1R20	1R2[illegible]	..	..	..	6R 0	6R 0
Wakefield (Kirkgate) dep	..	TC from Bridlington, dep. 2 20 p.m. (Tables 105 and 87)	4 30	TC from Cleethorpes, dep. 2 0 p.m. (Tables 67 and 89)	..	5 8	5 8	5 8	..	5F37	5U37	..	6 12	6 58	6 58	..	9 3	..	..		..	..	..	..	..	..	..	..	..	..	..	..	..
" (Westgate) "	..		4 46		5 10	5 18	5 31	5 46	5 52	5 58	5 50	6 13	6 28	7 15	7 32	8 20	9 30	10 7	1026		1026	1030	11 [illegible]	2 57	3 0	..	5 58	6 [illegible]	..	7 34	..	10 6	1010
Alverthorpe	..		..		TC from King's Cross. Via Ardsley	5 22	TC from King's Cross. Via Ardsley	Via Ardsley	..	..	5 54	TC from King's Cross. Via Ardsley	..	..	7 36	TC from King's Cross. Via Ardsley	9 34	TC from King's Cross. Via Ardsley	..		TC from King's Cross. Via Ardsley	1034	..	TC from King's Cross Via Ardsley	..	..	TC from King's Cross Via Ardsley	..	..	..	..	TC from King's Cross Via Ardsley	..
Ossett	..		4 57			5 30			..	..	6 2		6 40	7 27	7 43		9 41		..			1041	11 18		3 8	..		6 9	..	7 42	..		1018
Earlsheaton	..		..			5 34			..	..	6 6		..	..	7 47		9 45		..			1045	..		..	..		..	..	..	..		..
Dewsbury	..		5 4			5 38			..	..	6 11		6 47	7 34	7 50		9 48		..			1048	11 29		3 13	..		6 14	..	7 49	..		1023
Batley Carr	..		..			5 40			..	..	6 13		..	..	..		..		..			..	..		..	..		..	..	..	..		..
Batley	..		5 10			5T44			..	..	6 17		6 53	7 40	7 54		9 52		..			1052	11 34		3 17	..		6 18	..	7 53	..		1027
Upper Batley [stall	..		..			5T48			..	..	6 21		TC from Skegness dep. 3 10 p.m. (Table 57)	TC from Skegness, dep. 3 44 p.m. (Table 57)	7 58		9 56		..			..	..		..	..		..	..	..	..		..
Howden Clough, for Bir-	..		..			5T52			..	..	6 25				8 2		10 0		..			..	..		..	..		..	..	..	..		..
Lofthouse A	..		..			..			5 58	..	..				..		..		..			..	..		..	..		..	..	..	..		..
Ardsley	4 59		..			..			6 3	..	..				..		..		..			..	..		..	..		..	..	..	..		..
Tingley	..		..			..			6 7	..	..				..		..		..			..	..		..	..		..	..	..	..		..
Morley	5 6		..		5 25	..	5 48	6 1	6 11	6 13	..	6 28			..	8 35	..	1022	1041		1041	..	..		..	..		..	..	..	..		..
Gildersome	..		..		..	..	..	..	6 15	..	..	..			..	..	..	..	..		..	..	..		..	..	..	..	..	..	..	..	..
Drighlington B	..		..		..	5T58	..	..	6 19	..	6 32	..			8 8	..	10 6	..	..		..	11 3	..		..	..	..	..	..	..	..	..	..
Birkenshaw and Tong	..		..		..	6T 2	..	..	..	..	6 36	..			8 12	..	1010	..	..		..	11 8	..		..	..	..	..	..	..	..	..	..
Dudley Hill	..		..		..	6T 6	..	..	..	..	6 40	..			8 16	..	1014	..	..		..	1111	..		..	..	..	..	..	..	..	..	..
Laisterdyke	..		..		..	6T11	..	..	..	..	6 45	..			8 21	..	1019	..	..		..	1116	11 54	..	3 36	..	..	6 37	..	8 13	..	..	1046
St. Dunstan's arr	..		..		..	6T14	..	..	..	..	6 48	..			8 24	..	..	..	..		..	..	..	..	..	..	..	..	..	..	..	..	..
Bradford (Exchange) "	5 25		5 33		5 44	6T16	6 7	6 21	..	6 32	6 51	6 49	7 18	8 5	8 27	8 54	1024	1041	11 0		11 0	1121	11 59	3 28	3 41	..	6 29	6 42	..	8 19	..	1037	1051

A Lofthouse and Outwood
B Drighlington and Adwalton
C or **C** Saturdays only. Runs until 27th September inclusive
D Saturdays only. Runs 5th July to 27th September inclusive
E Except Saturdays
F Fridays only
F Except 4th October
H Saturdays only. Runs until 5th July and from 6th to 27th September inclusive
K Saturdays only. Runs 12th July to 30th August inclusive
K Except Saturday nights. Depart 10 55 on Friday night and 11 0 on Sunday night.
L Mondays and Saturdays
P Arr. 4 minutes *earlier*
R Restaurant Car
S or S Saturdays only
T 3 minutes later on Saturdays
TC Through Carriages
U Arr. 6 minutes *earlier*
V 10 minutes later on Saturdays
Z Change at Laisterdyke
† Arr. 3 minutes *earlier*

For **OTHER TRAINS**

BETWEEN	TABLE
Wakefield and Batley	92
Wakefield and Lofthouse	87
Wakefield and Ardsley	89
Wakefield and Tingley	92
Ardsley and Bradford	93
Laisterdyke and Bradford	91

Right:
With Wakefield Westgate in the background, Ivatt-designed 'N1' 0-6-2T No 69463 takes the Bradford slow service past Balne Lane. The train will diverge here from the main Wakefield-Leeds/Bradford line to travel via Dewsbury and Batley. This ex-Great Northern line was closed to passenger services on 7 September 1964. *Kenneth Field*

Table 90— *continued*

BRADFORD (Exchange), ARDSLEY, BATLEY, DEWSBURY, and WAKEFIELD

Week Days

Miles		a.m		a.m	a.m		a.m	a.m C		a.m L	a.m	a.m	a.m	a.m C
	Bradford (Exchange) dep	5 37	..	..	6 10	..	..	6 50	Through Train to Scarborough (Londesbro' Rd.) arr. 9 20 a.m. (Tables 87 and 109)	7 10	7 25	7 50	..	8 17
½	St. Dunstan's	5 40	..	..	6 13	..	..	..		Via Ardsley	..	7 53	..	..
2	Laisterdyke	5 45	..	..	6 19	..	..	..			..	7 58	..	..
3½	Dudley Hill	5 50	..	..	6 24	..	..	..			..	8 3	..	..
5¼	Birkenshaw and Tong	5 55	..	..	6 29	..	..	..			..	8 8	..	..
6¼	Drighlington B	5 59	..	6 8	6 33	..	6 45	..			..	8 12	8 20	..
8	Gildersome	..	..	6 11	..	..	6 48	..			TC to King's Cross	..	8 23	..
9¾	Morley	..	..	6 15	..	..	6 52	7 9		7 31	..	..	8 27	..
10¾	Tingley	..	..	6 19	..	..	6 55	..			..	..	8 30	..
12¼	Ardsley	..	..	6 24	..	..	7 7	7 13			..	..	8 45	..
14¼	Lofthouse A (stall)	..	..	6U33	..	..	7 12	..			..	..	8 50	..
8½	Howden Clough, for Bir-	6 2	..	..	6 36	..	Arr. Ardsley 6 59 a.m.	..		TC to King's Cross	..	8 15	Arr. Ardsley 8 34 a.m.	..
9	Upper Batley	6 5	..	..	6 39	..		..			..	8 18		..
10½	**Batley**	6 8	..	..	6 42	..		..			7 48	8 21		8 40
11	Batley Carr	..	..	..	6 45	..		..			..	8 24		..
11¼	**Dewsbury**	6 12	..	..	6 48	..		..			7 53	8 27		8B47
12½	Earlsheaton	6 15	..	..	6 51	..		..			..	8 30		..
14	**Ossett**	6 20	..	..	6 55	..		..			8 1	8 34		8 53
16½	Alverthorpe	6 27	..	..	7 0	..		..			..	8 39		..
18	**Wakefield** (Wes'gte) arr	6 34	..	6 37	7 4	..	7 16	..		7 43	8 8	8 45	8 54	9 2
18½	" (Kirkgate) "	6 38	..	..	7 13	..	..	..		..	..	..	9 5	9 19
196½	89 London (King'sC.) arr	..	..	..	..	..	..	..		11R35	12R12	..	..	..

		a.m S	a.m	a.m	a.m C		a.m	a.m P	a.m D		p.m S	p.m P	p.m	p.m		p.m
Bradford (Exchange) dep	Through Train on Saturdays (12th July to 30th August inclusive) to Skegness, arr. 12 4 p.m. (Table 57)	8 38	..	9 30	9 38	Through Train to Bridlington, arr. 12 25 p.m. (Tables 87 and 108)	9 45	1125	11 36	..	..	12 4	1223	12 35	..	2 5
St. Dunstan's		8 41	..	Via Ardsley	..		TC to King's Cross (Mons., Fris. & Sats.)	..	..	..	..	Via Ardsley	Via Ardsley	12 38	..	2 8
Laisterdyke		8 46	..		..		..	1131	11 44	..	..			12 43	..	2 14
Dudley Hill		..	..		..		..	1136	11 49	..	..			12 48	..	2 19
Birkenshaw and Tong		8 52	..		..		..	1141	11 54	..	..			12 53	..	2 24
Drighlington B		8 56	9 20		..		..	1145	11 58	..	12 5			12 57	..	2 28
Gildersome		..	9 23		..		..	..	..	..	12 8			..	..	..
Morley		..	9 27	9 51	10 0		..	..	..	..	12 12	1225	1244	..	..	..
Tingley		..	9 30		..		..	..	..	..	12 15		..	..	..	..
Ardsley		..	9 35		10 8		..	..	..	..	12 20		..	..	..	..
Lofthouse A (stall)		..	9 40		..		..	..	..	..	12 25		..	..	..	..
Howden Clough, for Bir-		..	..	TC to King's Cross	..		..	1148	12 1	..	..	TC to King's Cross	..	1 0	..	2 31
Upper Batley		9 1	..		..		..	1151	12 4	..	..		..	1 3	..	2 33
Batley		9 4	..		..		10 8	1154	12 7	..	..		..	1 6	..	2 36
Batley Carr		..	..		..		..	1157	12 10	..	..		..	1 9	..	..
Dewsbury		9 8	..		..		1013	12 0	12 13	..	..		..	1B14	..	2P46
Earlsheaton		..	..		..		..	12 3	12 16	..	..		..	1 17	..	2 49
Ossett		9 14	..		..		1021	12 8	12 21	..	..		..	1 21	..	2 55
Alverthorpe		..	..		..		..	1213	12 26	..	..		..	1 26	..	3 0
Wakefield (Wes'gte) arr		9 23	9 45	10 3	..		1028	1217	12 34	..	12 29	1238	1256	1 30	..	3 4
" (Kirkgate) "		9V38	10 0	10V28	..		..	..	..	..	..	..	1 22	2 12	..	3 16
89 London (King'sC.) arr		..	..	1R45	..		2R45	..	..	..	..	4 35	5R18	7HR46	..	7R46

Week Days—*continued*

	p.m	p.m E	p.m	p.m		p.m E	p.m	p.m	p.m E	p.m	p.m E		p.m	p.m R	p.m F	p.m	p.m
Bradford (Exchange) dep	2 50	..	3 42	4 18	..	..	5 4	5 11	..	5 50	..	..	7 40	8 57	8 57	9 40	1045
St. Dunstan's	Via Ardsley	..	3 45	..	..	..	..	5 14	..	5Z28	..	..	7 43	9 0	9 0	..	..
Laisterdyke		..	3 50	4 24	..	..	..	5 19	..	5 57	..	..	7H51	9B 7	9B 7	..	1051
Dudley Hill		..	3 55	4 29	..	..	TC to King's Cross	5 24	..	6 2	..	..	7 56	9 12	9 12	..	1056
Birkenshaw and Tong		..	4 0	4 34	..	..		5 29	..	6 7	..	..	8 1	9 17	9 17	..	11 1
Drighlington B		3 35	4 4	4 38	..	5 0		5 33	5 37	6 11	6 30	..	8 6	9 21	9 21	..	11 5
Gildersome		3 38	..	..	..	5 3		..	5 40	..	6 33	..	..	..	..	..	..
Morley	3 11	3 42	..	..	..	5 7		..	5 44	..	6 37	..	..	..	..	10 1	..
Tingley		3 45	..	..	..	5 10		..	5 47	..	6 40	..	..	..	..	..	..
Ardsley		4 10	..	..	..	5 15		..	5 52	..	6 44	..	..	..	..	10 7	..
Lofthouse A (stall)	TC to King's Cross	4 15	..	..	..	5 21		..	5 58	..	6 50	..	..	..	..	..	..
Howden Clough for Bir-		Arr. Ardsley 3 49 p.m.	4 7	4 41	..	..	..	5 36	..	6 14	..	..	8 9	9 24	9 24	..	..
Upper Batley			4 10	4 44	..	..	..	5 39	..	6 17	..	..	8 12	9 27	9 27	..	..
Batley			4 14	4 48	..	..	5 27	5 43	..	6 20	..	..	8 16	9 30	9 31	..	1115
Batley Carr			4 17	4 51	..	..	..	5 46	..	6 23	..	..	..	..	..	..	..
Dewsbury			4 21	4B56	..	..	5 32	5 49	..	6 26	..	..	8P26	9 35	9B37	..	1120
Earlsheaton	..		4 24	4 59	..	..	..	5 52	..	6 29	..	..	8 29	9 39	9 41	..	..
Ossett	..		4 29	5 4	..	..	..	5 59	..	6 33	..	..	8 35	9 43	9B47	..	1127
Alverthorpe	..		4 36	5 11	..	..	..	6 6	..	6 40	..	..	8B42	9 48	9 52	..	..
Wakefield (Wes'gte) arr	3 24	4 19	4 40	5 15	..	5 25	5 48	6 10	6 2	6 44	6 54	..	8 46	9 52	9 59	1015	1134
" (Kirkgate) "	..	..	..	5 19	..	..	6 7	..	6 7	..	..	..	..	..	..	1039	..
89 London (King'sC.) arr	7R46	..	..	..	..	..	10R 2	..	..	..	..	..	..	..	..	3a45	..

Sundays

	a.m	a.m	a.m		p.m	p.m	p.m	p.m	p.m	p.m	p.m	p.m	p.m	
Bradford (Exchange) dep	9 13	9 40	1040	..	1220	1 10	4 20	4 48	5 8	7 0	8 57	9 13	9 40	..
St. Dunstan's	..	Via Ardsley	..	..	..	TC to King's Cross Via Ardsley	..	TC to King's Cross Via Ardsley	TC to King's Cross	..	TC to King's Cross Via Ardsley	..	..	..
Laisterdyke	9 20		1046	..	1227		4 27			7 6		9 20	..	..
Dudley Hill	..		..	..	..		..			..		..	..	..
Birkenshaw and Tong	..		..	..	..		..			..		..	..	..
Drighlington B	..		..	..	..		..			..		..	..	..
Gildersome	..		..	..	..		..			..		..	..	..
Morley	..		..	..	..		..			..		..	..	..
Tingley	..		..	..	..		..			..		..	..	..
Ardsley	..		..	..	..		..			..		..	..	..
Lofthouse A (stall)	..		..	..	..		..			..		..	..	..
Howden Clough for Bir-	..		..	..	..		..			..		..	..	..
Upper Batley	..		..	..	..		..			..		..	..	..
Batley	9 36	TC to King's Cross	11 4	..	1243		4 43		Via Ardsley	7 24		9 36	..	..
Batley Carr	..		..	..	..		..			..		..	..	..
Dewsbury	9 41		11 8	..	1248	..	4 48	..		7 28	..	9 41	..	..
Earlsheaton	..		..	..	..		..			..		..	..	..
Ossett	9 48		1115	..	1255	..	4 55	..		7 35	..	9 48	..	..
Alverthorpe	..		..	..	..		..			..		..	..	..
Wakefield (Wes'gte) arr	9 55	1012	1123	..	1 2	1 42	5 2	5 20	5 40	7 42	9 29	9 58	1015	..
" (Kirkgate) "	..	..	..	..	1 7	..	..	..	..	..	..	1039	1039	..
89 London (King'sC.) arr	3R25	3R25	5R30	..	..	6R43	9 30	9 30	10R25	..	2a 0	3a45	3a45	..

A Lofthouse and Outwood
a a.m.
B Drighlington and Adwalton
B Arr. 3 minutes *earlier*
C Saturdays only. Runs until 27th September inclusive
D Except Fris. and Sats.

E or E Except Saturdays
F Fridays only
H Arr. 4 minutes *earlier*
L Mondays and Saturdays
N Arrives 7 15 p.m. on Saturdays
P Fridays and Saturdays
P Arr. 7 minutes *earlier*

R Except Fridays
R Restaurant Car
S Saturdays only
TC Through Carriages
U Arr. 5 mins. *earlier*
V Sats. only. Runs 5th July to 27th September inclusive
Z Change at Laisterdyke

For **OTHER TRAINS**

BETWEEN	TABLE
Bradford and Laisterdyke	91
Bradford and Ardsley	93
Tingley and Wakefield	92
Ardsley and Wakefield	89
Lofthouse and Wakefield	87
Batley and Wakefield	92

Above:
The ex-GNR station at Dewsbury, Central, was predominantly served by Wakefield-Dewsbury-Bradford Exchange local services, one of which, headed by 'N1' No 69440 is seen in the station. Dewsbury Central station closed to passenger services, along with the rest of the route, in September 1964.
Kenneth Field

Below:
A Bradford-Dewsbury-Wakefield local, in the charge of 'N1' No 69434, is seen working up the gradient between Dewsbury Central and Headfield Junction.
Kenneth Field

Above right:
One of the last duties to be undertaken by a 'Jubilee' in BR ownership was performed by No 45562 *Alberta* on 28 October 1967 when the locomotive was rostered to work a Manchester Railway Society/Severn Valley Railway Society special out of Normanton. The locomotive makes a fine sight as it departs from Normanton en route back to Birmingham.
Dr L. A. Nixon

Below right:
'Black 5' No 44672 steams away from Normanton with a train of empty mineral wagons from the West Riding to Lancashire on 28 October 1967. *John H. Bird*

45562

Top:
On 30 April 1953 'Black 5' No 44782 heads out of Normanton station with the 1.55pm York-Liverpool Exchange service. *Ian Allan Library*

Above:
'Jubilee' No 45739 *Ulster*, newly acquired by Wakefield MPD, is seen entering Castleford Central with a Wakefield-Scarborough excursion in August 1964. *P. Cookson*

Right:
Wakefield-allocated Fairburn 2-6-4T No 41252 departs from Wakefield Kirkgate (visible in the background) with a local service to Sowerby Bridge along the Calder Valley. Local services on this route were withdrawn in January 1970. *Kenneth Field*

Below:
'B1' No 61017 *Bushbuck* departs from Burton Salmon with a three-coach train for Wakefield via Castleford and Normanton. The lines on the right head towards Pontefract and thence to Rotherham and Sheffield. The ex-NER station at Burton Salmon, visible through the road bridge, closed to passenger services on 14 September 1959 although the junction remains. *Kenneth Field*

Goole (53E)
Allocation as at 1959

Class 1F	41661, 41797, 41855
Class 4	42436
Class 2	46407, 46408, 46409, 46414
Class 0F	51222, 51241, 51244
Class 3F	52154, 52244, 52252, 52305, 52319
Class WD	90094, 90186, 90213, 90228, 90260, 90262, 90265, 90281, 90300, 90478, 90531

Above:
Although perceived as a land-locked county, the West Riding stretched as far east as Goole and the docks there, thus, fall into the area covered by this book. The docks developed rapidly in the mid-19th century under the patronage of the Lancashire & Yorkshire Railway primarily for the shipment of coal. It is, therefore, appropriate that an ex-L&YR 0-4-0ST, No 51244 (one of a class introduced in 1891 to a design by Aspinall), is seen shunting at the docks with, on the right, rakes of loaded and empty coal wagons.
D. Holmes

Above right:
The southbound 'White Rose' express departs from Wakefield Westgate en route for Doncaster and London behind 'A1' Pacific No 60148 *Aboyeur*. *A. M. Ross*

Below right:
On 18 March 1967 Fairburn 2-6-4T No 42196 hauled the through coaches for Bradford off the 10.20am express from King's Cross. The train is seen passing Outwood, near Wakefield, *en route* for its destination.
J. S. Hancock

60148

42196

Top:
With the coaling stage of Wakefield shed prominent in the background, 'Austerity' 2-8-0 No 90467 lifts a southbound train of coal empties out of Wakefield in April 1960.
Ken Smith

Above:
Seen at Normanton on 21 July 1963, Thompson 'B1' No 61369 hauls an oil tank train past the photographer. Normanton, once a refreshment halt on the main line to Scotland, remained an important junction, particularly for freight, although bypassed by East Coast main line trains following the opening of the route north from Doncaster.
R. A. Panting

Huddersfield

The town of Huddersfield was the focus for a number of early railway schemes, but it was not until August 1847 that the first railway link, north to Heaton Lodge Junction, was opened. The line approached Huddersfield over a viaduct almost 700yd in length. The next stage in the town's railway development came with the opening of the line through to Stalybridge via the three-mile tunnel at Standedge, which opened on 1 August 1849. These two lines formed part of the London & North Western Railway's main line from Manchester to Leeds. South of Huddersfield, the Huddersfield & Sheffield Junction Railway, later to form part of the Lancashire & Yorkshire Railway, was to open its line to Penistone on 1 July 1850. The L&YR was to reach its southern lines via running powers over the LNWR route. Apart from a minor incursion by the Midland Railway, which opened a goods-only branch to Newtown goods depot in November 1910, Huddersfield's railway history was to be dominated by the LNWR and L&YR.

The station constructed at Huddersfield, begun in 1846 and completed in 1850 to a design by J. P. Pritchett, is, without doubt, the finest station constructed in the West Riding in architectural terms and, today, is rightfully listed. Apart from the central portico, with its eight columns, the station also boasted two separate sets of offices, one for the LNWR and the other for the L&YR situated at the north and south ends of the building respectively. The main station building was acquired by Huddersfield Corporation in 1968 to mark the centenary of the borough's incorporation and has been fully restored and cleaned since then.

In addition to the main lines, there were also a number of short branches in the area. These were the L&YR branches to Holmfirth (opened on 1 July 1850), to Meltham (opened to passenger services on 5 July 1869) and Clayton West (opened on 1 September 1879), as well as the LNWR branch to Kirkburton which opened on 7 October 1867). The increasing level of traffic heading north of Huddersfield led to the widening of the viaduct north of the station in the 1880s and to the LNWR's construction of the 'New' line to Leeds, via Liversedge and Cleckheaton. This line was opened to passenger services on 1 October 1900.

As the LNWR and L&YR merged in 1922, prior to the Grouping, all the local lines in the Huddersfield area passed to the LMS already under single ownership. There was to be little real change in the pattern of services through until the post-Nationalisation period, with, for example, services over the ex-L&YR

Below:
The branch to Holmfirth from Brockholes on the Huddersfield-Penistone route was opened in July 1950. The 1¾ mile line had one intermediate station, Thongs Bridge, and trains took six minutes to trundle their way from Brockholes. Whilst services were not particularly frequent, it was possible to travel from Holmfirth on through services to both Bradford and Halifax. In August 1955 Ivatt 2-6-2T No 41250 awaits departure from the branch terminus. Passenger services over the line were to be withdrawn on 2 November 1959, whilst freight trains ceased to operate on 3 May 1965. *Real Photographs*

branches south of Huddersfield running, normally, through Huddersfield and on to Halifax and Bradford.

With the exception of two sections of line, the ex-Midland freight-only line to Newtown (which had been linked to the LNWR line at Red Doles Junction in 1923 with the section north to Mirfield Junction closing in 1937) and the Kirkburton branch (which had lost its passenger services in 1930), the entire local network passed to BR in 1948. However, as elsewhere, it was not to be long before the harsh economic reality of the 1950s led to closures. The first to close to passenger services was the branch to Meltham (on 23 May 1949; it survived for freight until 5 April 1965), to be followed by the Holmfirth branch (on 2 November 1959; freight again lasted longer being withdrawn on 3 May 1965) and, finally in the steam era, the Leeds 'New' line which lost its services on 2 August 1965. The final branch in the area, that to Clayton West, was to survive the withdrawal of steam and was to close finally in the early 1980s. Ironically, with the construction of the Kirklees Light Railway along the trackbed, this is now the only section of line in the area to see regular steam operation.

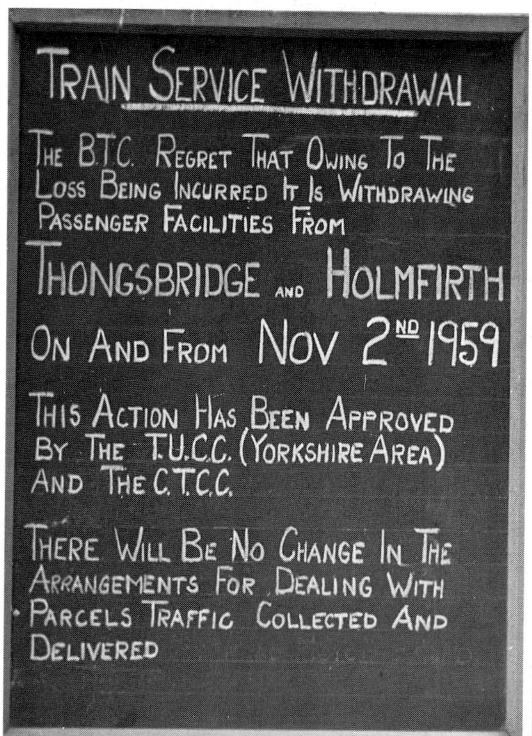

TRAIN SERVICE WITHDRAWAL
THE B.T.C. REGRET THAT OWING TO THE LOSS BEING INCURRED IT IS WITHDRAWING PASSENGER FACILITIES FROM
THONGSBRIDGE AND HOLMFIRTH
ON AND FROM NOV 2ND 1959
THIS ACTION HAS BEEN APPROVED BY THE T.U.C.C. (YORKSHIRE AREA) AND THE C.T.C.C.
THERE WILL BE NO CHANGE IN THE ARRANGEMENTS FOR DEALING WITH PARCELS TRAFFIC COLLECTED AND DELIVERED

Left:
Typical motive power on the Holmfirth branch in its later years were the Ivatt 2-6-2Ts introduced in 1946. One of the class, No 41276, is seen at the buffer stops at Holmfirth whilst running round its train. *Geoff Lumb*

Below left:
A sign of the times: the chalked notice advising passengers that the passenger service was being withdrawn; more official, printed notices, were also produced. *Geoff Lumb*

Above right:
Penistone was the junction where the ex-L&YR line from Huddersfield met the ex-Great Central lines from Manchester, Sheffield and Barnsley. Fairburn 2-6-4T No 42112 has just arrived at Penistone with a through service from Bradford to Sheffield in April 1950. The train took on average 1hr 20min for the 26-mile trip from Bradford; it would take a minimum of a further 40min to reach Sheffield (Victoria) — a further 13 miles on. *Real Photographs*

Below right:
Clayton West was the terminus of the ex-L&YR branch from Shepley & Shelley on the Huddersfield-Penistone line. Clayton West Station Cabin box was supplied by Saxby & Farmer in 1878. Seen here in the early 1960s, it still retained its L&YR nameboard. The box was eventually to be abolished on 22 January 1983 with the withdrawal of passenger services over the branch. *Real Photographs*

Huddersfield (55G)
Allocation as at 1959

Class 4	42310, 42312, 42377, 42384, 42408, 42409, 42410, 42412, 42413, 42414
Class 5	73162, 73163, 73164, 73165, 73166
Class WD	90243, 90249, 90325, 90332, 90345, 90347, 90619, 90621, 90624, 90680, 90694

Top left:
The Meltham branch met the Huddersfield-Penistone line at Lockwood. Here we see No 45101 at the junction as its crew prepares to hand over the single-line token to the signalman at Lockwood No 2 box. Freight services over the line, despite the presence of the tractor factory, were withdrawn in April 1965. *Geoff Lumb*

Centre left:
The branch to Meltham was the first to be encountered south of Huddersfield on the ex-L&YR line to Penistone. Meltham was the first of the three ex-L&YR branches to lose its passenger services — on 23 May 1949 — but was to survive as a freight branch much longer. The primary traffic flow was from the tractor works of David Brown and a consignment from the factory is pictured departing from the terminus behind 'Black 5' No 45101. *Geoff Lumb*

Below left:
Stocksmoor was (and is) one of the intermediate stations on the ex-L&YR line from Huddersfield to Penistone. Here a Fairburn-designed 2-6-4T heads a three-coach train into the station with a northbound train. Note the LMS pattern station nameboards. *Roy Brook*

Above right:
'Black 5' No 45079 and 'Royal Scot' No 46144 *The Honourable Artillery Company* double-head a midday Newcastle-Liverpool express through Slaithwaite, on the ex-LNWR main line from Huddersfield to Manchester, on 14 March 1952. *J. D. Sutcliffe*

Below right:
'B1' 4-6-0 No 61166 pulls into the L&YR platforms at Penistone with a Barnsley-Doncaster local service. The locomotive has run round the train on the viaduct to the north of the station. *Kenneth Field*

45079

61166

Above:
At 3 miles 66yd, Standedge Tunnel is one of the longest in the country. Here 'Black 5' No 45285 approaches the eastern end of the tunnel with the Saturdays Only 12.30pm service from Leeds to Manchester on 5 August 1967. *M. Mitchell*

Above right:
Having just passed through Marsden station, on the ex-LNWR main line from Manchester to Huddersfield, '8F' No 48182 heads east on 23 May 1964. *John K. Morton*

Below right:
Brockholes, on the Huddersfield-Penistone line, was the junction for the short branch to Holmfirth until the latter closed. Here an unidentified ex-LMS 2-6-4T waits in the southbound platform. *Roy Brook*

46182

Above:
On 28 October 1967 the Manchester Rail Travel Society and the Severn Valley Railway jointly organised a tour from Birmingham to Manchester and over various lines in the West Riding. Motive power for the excursion included 'Britannia' No 70013 *Oliver Cromwell*. The train is seen at Berry Brow heading south from Huddersfield *en route* to Penistone. *J. R. Hillier*

Below:
The Kirkburton branch of the LNWR opened in 1867. It was a relatively early casualty with passenger services being withdrawn on 28 July 1930. Freight services were, however, to last longer being finally withdrawn on 5 April 1965 with the exception of traffic to the ICI factory at Deighton, which lasted until 1971. 'Austerity' 2-8-0 No 90619 is seen with a short freight on the branch. *Geoff Lumb*

Above:
'Jubilee' No 45695 *Minotaur* approaches Huddersfield station from the north across the viaduct that gave the LNWR access to the town from the north. The viaduct had been widened in the 1880s as a result of increasing traffic.
Roy Brook

Right:
Passenger services were briefly resumed to Kirkburton on 2 May 1959 when a Railway Enthusiasts' Club special traversed the line (along with other West Riding routes). Motive power along the branch was provided by BR Standard Class 4 2-6-4T No 80044.
Geoff Lumb

Doncaster

If any one town could be said to have been a magnet for railway enthusiasts in the West Riding it was probably Doncaster. Not only did it act as a great junction, with lines radiating north to York, northwest to Leeds, northeast to Hull, east to the Lincolnshire coast, southeast towards Lincoln, south towards London and southwest towards Sheffield, it also possessed, in the Works, the most important of the ex-LNER workshops, where many of the most famous steam engines were constructed and where many were to be seen regularly under repair. At its peak it was possible to see locomotives from six of the pre-Grouping companies at the station.

Although Doncaster was a Roman city, its importance came really from the development of the Great Northern Railway. The GNR line from Retford to Askern Junction (just north of Doncaster where the new GNR met the metals of the NER and L&YR) opened on 4 September 1849. The GNR soon took over the operation of the L&YR's line from Askern to Knottingley and Leeds (although this lost its importance once the direct line to Wakefield was completed under the aegis of the West Riding & Grimsby Joint in 1866). Also arriving in Doncaster in 1849 was the South Yorkshire, Doncaster & Goole Railway, which was later to form part of the Manchester, Sheffield & Lincolnshire Railway's route to the east coast. The MS&LR was later to become the Great Central, a line which was to carry huge quantities of coal for its newly constructed docks at Immingham through Doncaster.

It was in 1851 that the board of the GNR selected Doncaster as the base for its new locomotive workshops, replacing the company's existing facility at Boston. The works were to expand rapidly, reaching some 200 acres by the start of the 20th century. It was from these workshops that many of the greatest and most famous steam locomotives of both the Great Northern and LNER were to emerge; for 30 years, from 1911 until his death in 1941 Nigel Gresley was to design and Doncaster was to build a whole range of classic steam locomotives, perhaps reaching their peak with the streamlined 'A4s' of the mid-1930s. Steam locomotive manufacture continued at the Plant through until October 1957, when the last BR Standard Class 4 2-6-0 No 76114 was completed.

1866 was to be another important year with the opening of the direct link to Wakefield and the first stage of the lines that would ultimately link the town to both Goole and Grimsby. The following year the line to

Below:
South of Doncaster, the West Riding stretched as far as Bawtry on the East Coast main line. On 31 August 1954, just south of Doncaster station, 'V2' 2-6-2 No 60982 was photographed hauling a Newcastle-King's Cross express. The journey from Newcastle had probably taken over two hours and there were still over another three hours before the train's ultimate destination would be reached.
Brian Morrison

Gainsborough was opened; eventually this was to form part of the Great Northern & Great Eastern Joint line, a route which was to bring the sixth pre-Grouping railway (the GER) into Doncaster. A seventh pre-Grouping company, the ill-fated Hull & Barnsley Railway, also served the district but never directly ran into Doncaster. Designed to provide competition for the coal traffic to the Humber ports, the H&BR opened to Cudworth in July 1885. Later extensions saw Wrangbrook (just north of Doncaster) become a 'major' junction with lines to Denaby and Wath opening in 1894 and 1902 respectively. Although freight was the primary rationale for the line, passenger services were also introduced; these were, however, short-lived. The last were withdrawn in 1932. Freight survived, in part, until the late 1960s.

Apart from the disappearance of the Hull & Barnsley, the Doncaster area escaped relatively unscathed from the closures of the 1950s and 1960s. The original Knottingley-Askern line had lost its passenger services in September 1948, but the line remained open for coal traffic and for diverted passenger trains thereafter. There has been the inevitable rationalisation, particularly of duplicate lines and of lines serving now-closed collieries, but Doncaster was in the 1960s, and remains 30 years on, a major railway junction.

Above:
With Nationalisation, many of the traditional barriers disappeared and locomotives started to appear in unfamiliar places. In November 1954 ex-LMS No 40061, one of the Fowler-designed 2-6-2Ts introduced in 1930, was at Doncaster Works in the company of a more usual resident, Gresley-designed 'O2' 2-8-0 No 63959. *Real Photographs*

Below:
Although the East Coast main line skirted the West Riding north of York, it was only south of Selby that the line crossed the county boundary. Doncaster was, consequently, the major point on the route within the county. On Sunday 17 June 1956 the SLS (Midland Area) organised a tour to Doncaster Works from Birmingham (New Street), Derby and Nottingham. The train is seen at Doncaster behind 'Compound' 4-4-0 No 40928. *Real Photographs*

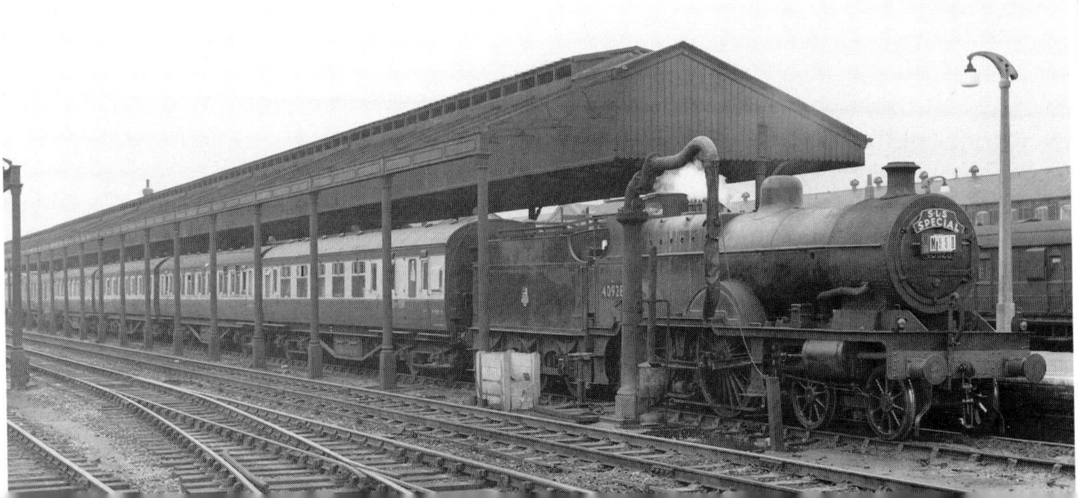

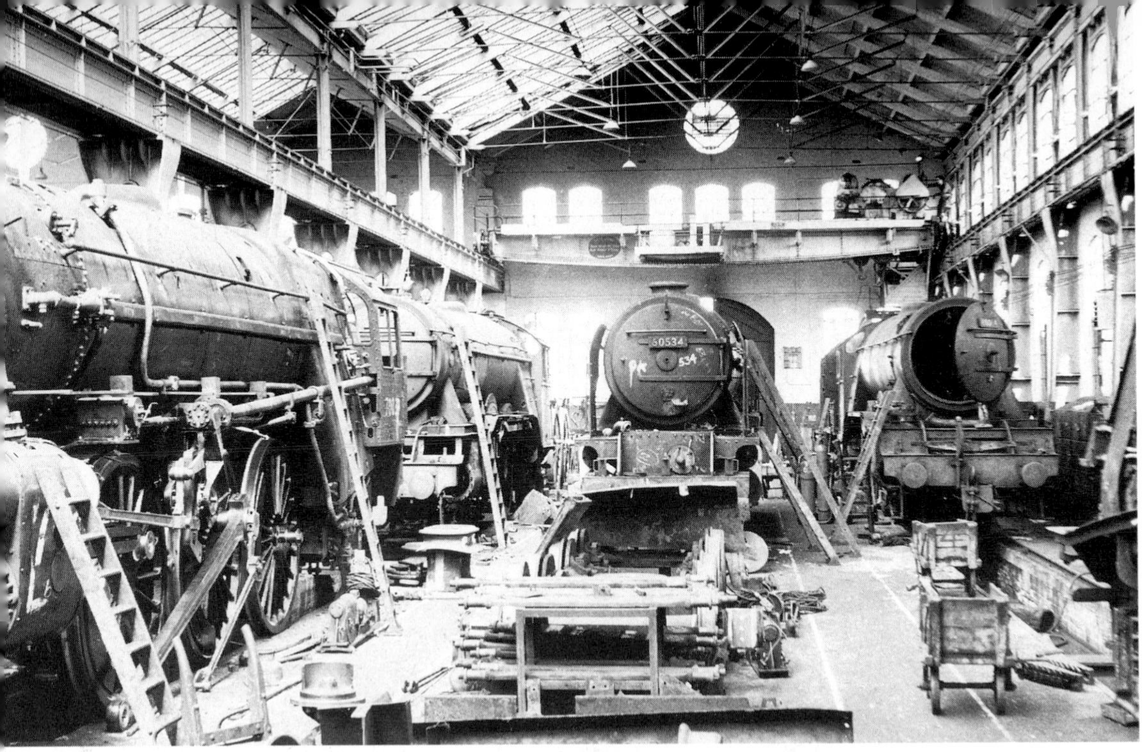
60534

68974

Above left:
There was only one major locomotive works established in the West Riding — but what a works it was! Doncaster was selected by the Great Northern Railway as the location of the company's locomotive works and from its opening in 1853 it was to produce a succession of classic locomotives that graced the East Coast main line. Apart from the construction of new locomotives, the works was also engaged in the overhaul of others. Inevitably, the works acted as a magnet for enthusiasts and numerous tours and excursions featured the 'Plant' as the centre piece of the day's activities. On this occasion, 'A2' Pacific No 60534 *Irish Elegance* is seen in the company of 'Britannia' No 70039 *Sir Christopher Wren* and 'A3' No 60064 *Tagalie.*
Brian Morrison

Below left:
The 'J50' 0-6-0Ts were familiar sights over the ex-GN lines in the West Riding for many years. No 68974 is seen at Doncaster shed on 31 August 1954. The 'J50/3s', of which No 68974 was one, were introduced in 1926, as a modified version of Gresley's earlier design. *Brian Morrison*

Above:
There was only one 4-6-4 tender locomotive inherited by British Railways in 1948 — Gresley's streamlined Class W1 No 60700. Built in 1937, the locomotive was substantially a rebuild of Gresley's earlier experimental high-pressure four-cylinder compound which dated from 1929. This unique locomotive is seen in Doncaster shed on 31 August 1954. It was withdrawn in 1959. *Brian Morrison*

Above:
Thompson-designed 'B1' No 61365 waits at Doncaster with the ECS for the 9am service to Grimsby on 31 August 1954. From its 36A (Doncaster) shedplate — clearly visible on the smokebox — No 61365 was not far from home.
Brian Morrison

Left:
A total of 70 'B16' 4-6-0s were built by the NER and LNER between 1920 and 1924 to a design of Sir Vincent Raven. A total of 69 passed to BR in 1948, but, of these, 17 had been rebuilt by Gresley during the 1930s and seven more by Thompson during the following decade. The Gresley rebuild included the fitting of replacement Walschaerts motion. One of the locomotives modified to Gresley's design, No 61437, is seen on Doncaster shed on 31 August 1954. The shed plate (50A), visible on the smokebox door, records that the locomotive was based at York at this time.
Brian Morrison

Above:
Blaydon-based 'K2' 2-6-0 No 62022 is seen passing Balby Junction, south of Doncaster, with a northbound freight on 31 August 1954. *Brian Morrison*

Right:
Introduced in 1926, a total of 289 of Gresley's 'J39' 0-6-0s were constructed. No 64721 is pictured at Balby Junction on 31 August 1954 with a freight.
Brian Morrison

Top:
Introduced in 1911, a total of 110 'J6' 0-6-0s were constructed to a design of Nigel Gresley between then and 1922. All passed to BR in 1948 and Colwick-allocated No 64235 is seen immediately north of Doncaster station on 31 August 1954 with a (very) short freight. At this time the class was intact; withdrawals, however, started the following year and all had been taken out of service by 1962. *Brian Morrison*

Above:
'B16' No 61460 heads south towards Doncaster on 31 August 1954 with a freight. Note the trolleybus overhead on the road overbridge. This was the Doncaster Corporation's Bentley route, which was converted to bus operation on 12 February 1956 in connection with road works in the area. The rest of Doncaster's small trolleybus system was replaced by buses between 1961 and 1963. *Brian Morrison*

Above right:
Class K3 No 61903 heads through Stainforth & Hatfield with a down freight in April 1961. Note that the BR totem on the down platform records the station as 'Stainforth' alone. *John C. Baker*

Below right:
Stainforth & Hatfield, north of Doncaster, on the Doncaster-Hull line, is an important railway junction with the main ex-Great Central route heading east towards the North Sea ports of Grimsby and Immingham and with a line heading west to Adwick Junction to enable trains from the West Riding to avoid Doncaster. Class O4/3 No 63744 is seen leaving the up sidings at Stainforth with a westbound ballast train in April 1961. *John C. Baker*

61903

Top:
Class O2/2 No 63939, one of a class introduced in 1921 to a design by Gresley, is seen at Doncaster shed on 23 May 1959. This class was a development of No (6)3921 built in 1918, which represented Gresley's first three-cylinder design. The prototype locomotive, which was withdrawn in 1948 and never received its BR number, differed from the production batch in having inclined cylinders. A total of 66 production 'O2s' were built between 1921 and 1934 and all were withdrawn between 1960 and 1963.
Brian Morrison

Above:
Arguably one of the most famous steam locomotives ever constructed in Britain was No 60103 *Flying Scotsman,* which is pictured in front of the coaling stage at Doncaster shed on 23 May 1959. One of the author's most enduring memories of steam in the West Riding is seeing *Flying Scotsman*, by then restored to its LNER livery and bearing the number 4472, rushing through the level crossing at Hall Lane (on the Bradford 'avoiding' line) with a special in 1969 during the period when No 4472 kept the flag of main line steam flying alone. *Brian Morrison*

Sheffield and District

The railway history of the Sheffield, Rotherham and Barnsley areas is dominated by the rivalry of two railway companies — the Midland and the Manchester, Sheffield & Lincolnshire (later Great Central). Examination of any historical railway map illustrates that parallel lines were built between Sheffield and Rotherham in the northeast, Sheffield and Chesterfield in the south and Sheffield and Barnsley in the northwest. This rivalry was to continue through to 1948 as the former passed to the LMS and the latter to the LNER. It was only after Nationalisation that the inevitable rationalisation took place.

The first railway to serve the district was the Sheffield & Rotherham Railway which opened in November 1838. Although its original stations at Sheffield Wicker and Rotherham Westgate have been long-closed, this line still forms the core of the line north from Sheffield. The North Midland line, with which the S&RR was linked, opened between Leeds and Derby in 1840. These two lines formed part of the Midland Railway when that company was established. The Midland line through Sheffield (later to form the main line) opened in 1870. The second company to enter Sheffield, the Sheffield, Ashton-under-Lyne & Manchester (the early MS&LR) opened in 1845; it was extended eastwards towards Gainsborough in 1849. Further north the first railway to reach Barnsley, a branch of the L&YR from Horbury, opened in 1850. The future GCR reached Barnsley from Mexborough in 1851 and from Penistone in 1854. The line from Stairfoot to Tinsley, via Chapeltown, opened in 1854 and a connection from Tinsley, via Rotherham, to Mexborough was opened in 1868.

Construction of lines continued through the remaining years of the 19th century and into the first decade of the 20th, as the rival railway companies sought to compete in the burgeoning freight from the region's coal mines and iron works; later lines included the MS&LR (later Great Central) route south through Chesterfield to Nottingham, the Lancashire, Derbyshire & East Coast Railway (also eventually owned by the Great Central but which brought Great Eastern trains to the city courtesy of running powers over the Midland) and the Sheffield District Railway which opened in 1892, 1897 and 1900 respectively. The consequence was that lines paralleled each other — often running within sight of the competition as along the lines

Below:
Whilst many of the services over the former Great Central lines in the West Riding had been revolutionised by the electrification of the Woodhead route, those heading east out of Sheffield over the MS&L main line continued to be steam-hauled. Class J11 No 64292 stands in the platform at Sheffield (Victoria) with a service to Nottingham (Victoria) in June 1956. Allocated to Staveley (38D) at this time, No 64292 was to be amongst the last of the Robinson-designed class to remain in service. Normally used for freight and shunting services, the class was also used, as in this case, on local passenger turns. *Real Photographs*

Millhouses (41C)
Allocation as at 1959

Class 3	40148
Class 4P	40907
Class 2	41209, 41245, 41246
Class 4	43032
'Jubilee'	45570 *New Zealand*, 45576 *Bombay*, 45590 *Travancore*, 45594 *Bhopal*, 45602 *British Honduras*, 45607 *Fiji*, 45609 *Gilbert and Ellice Islands*, 45654 *Hood*, 45656 *Cochrane*, 45664 *Nelson*, 45683 *Hogue*, 45725 *Repulse*
Class 2	46400, 46494
Class 5	73004, 73011, 73016, 73046, 73048, 73065, 73067 73073, 73155
Class 2	78022, 78023, 78024, 78025

Above:
Situated between Millhouses & Eccleshall and Heeley stations, Millhouses was one of several Midland Railway sheds serving the city of Sheffield. It was to remain under the ownership of the London Midland Region (as 19B) until 1958 when it was transferred to the Eastern Region, becoming 41C. The shed had an allocation of mainly ex-LMS and BR 'Standard' designs by 1959, including one '4P' 4-4-0 Compound No 40907. Millhouses was to be closed in 1962.
Real Photographs

serving Chapeltown — and this led to numerous places like Rotherham (Central and Masborough), Sheffield (Victoria and Midland) and Barnsley (Court House and Exchange) all possessing two stations.

The position was not to be resolved by the Grouping. Although the Midland and L&YR were to form part of the LMS, the Great Central and Hull & Barnsley both passed to the LNER. Both of the 'Big Four' companies remained active in the area and the services operated retained their traditional pattern until Nationalisation. This might not have been the case, however, except for the outbreak of World War 2. The LNER had plans in the 1930s for the electrification of this trans-Pennine route but, in the event, it was not until 1948 that the first construction work started. The work, with the building of a new tunnel at Woodhead, was virtually completed in 1954 and this allowed for the replacement of steam-hauled passenger services over the Sheffield (Victoria)-Manchester route by new electric services and the introduction of electric-hauled coal trains from Wath.

The introduction of the new electric services was perhaps the first indication in the region that steam haulage did not have a long-term future. Other indications that the Nationalised railways were undergoing change came with the gradual elimination of much of the duplicated network that BR inherited in 1948. Lines closed to passenger services included the ex-Great Central line from Barnsley to Sheffield via Chapeltown (on 7 December 1953), the original ex-Midland main line from Chesterfield to Rotherham Masborough (on 5 July 1954), Barnsley Court House (on 19 April 1960), the ex-Great Central route from Tinsley through Rotherham to Mexborough (on 5 September 1966) and the old Midland main line from Wath Road to Goose Hill Junction on 7 October 1968. This last named line was to reopen five years later but was to close again in the early 1980s. Even the electrified line was to succumb with passenger services between Hadfield and Penistone (and Penistone-Barnsley) being withdrawn on 5 January 1970. Sheffield Victoria was to eke out its final days with a tenuous DMU link to Huddersfield until this service was rerouted to run via the reopened line to Barnsley. Freight lines suffered less severely, although with the contraction of the local steel industry and later the closure of the majority of mines, many of the lines that had survived — such as the ex-GCR route towards Nottingham — have slowly disappeared.

Inevitably, with such a network of lines, Sheffield and district boasted a number of important steam sheds. However, the gradual elimination of steam and the construction of new depots (such as Tinsley) for the replacement diesel locomotives meant that many of the area's sheds closed relatively early: Millhouses in 1962; Grimesthorpe in 1961; Darnall in 1963; Canklow in 1965; Mexborough in 1964.

Right:
In June 1952 ex-LMS No 40193 is seen at Barnsley (Court House). Four years after Nationalisation the locomotive retains its 'LMS' legend on the sidetank, whilst the smokebox number shows its new identity. Barnsley (Court House) was originally a joint GCR/MR station, which opened on 2 May 1870. The station was to close in April 1960, when all services were diverted into the ex-L&YR Barnsley (Exchange) station. *Real Photographs*

Right:
The interior of Barnsley (Court House) station in April 1950 with ex-MR 0-4-4T No 58075 operating the 'Cudworth Motor'. The ex-MR route to Cudworth, where it met the ex-MR Sheffield-Leeds main line, was to close on 9 June 1958. There was only one intermediate station on the line at Monk Bretton and the trains took some eight minutes to make the five-mile trip. There were some 16 return workings per day. It is interesting to note how tidy the station platforms are; despite the apparent lack of litter bins there is no litter or debris visible. *Real Photographs*

64387
BARNSLEY
COURT HOUSE

Above left:
In June 1952 'J11' 0-6-0 No 64387 heads into Barnsley (Court House) with a Penistone-Doncaster service. Upon the closure of the line and station in 1960, services were transferred to Barnsley (Exchange). The Penistone-Barnsley service was discontinued on 5 January 1970, although services were later reinstated. *Real Photographs*

Below left:
A view looking east, in 1952, of the ex-GCR shed at Sheffield (Darnall). Scenes such as this, with numerous engines in light steam, were typical of the steam era locomotive shed. Darnall, with an allocation of more than 90 locomotives, housed a sizeable collection of ex-GC types, including latterly several of the 'Director' class 4-4-0s. It was finally to lose its steam allocation in June 1963.
Real Photographs

Above:
The concrete coaling stage was a familiar sight at most major loco sheds. Today, with very rare exceptions, it is an almost forgotten structure. Appropriately at an ex-Midland Railway shed — Sheffield (Grimesthorpe) code 19A — there are two ex-Midland locomotives — '2F' No 58225 and '3F' No 43388 — which were allocated to this shed. At this stage the shed was still under London Midland control; it was to be transferred to Eastern Region — as 41D — in 1958. It finally closed in 1961. *Brian Morrison*

Barnsley (41G)
Allocation as at 1959

Class O4	63612, 63623, 63656, 63659, 63669, 63697, 63704, 63718, 63726, 63727, 63731, 63763, 63802, 63824, 63836, 63883, 63904, 63907, 63911, 63913
Class J11	64376, 64403, 64404, 64417, 64425, 64442, 64452
Class J39	64828, 64902
Class C14	67445, 67448
Class N5	69268, 69320, 69342, 69343, 69354, 69370

Above:
Trafford Park-allocated 'Britannia' No 70038 *Robin Hood* is seen passing Woodhouse station (just east of Sheffield on the ex-Great Central route) on 8 June 1960 with the Liverpool-Harwich boat train. By this date the service was a regular duty for 'Britannias'. In the background can be seen the electrification masts of the 1,500V dc Sheffield-Wath scheme; Woodhouse represented the terminus of the electrified lines on the route towards Retford.
G. Newall

Above:
Stanier 'Black 5' No 45073 is pictured departing from Sheffield (Midland) on 9 May 1966 with the 5.30pm service to Manchester. *Dr L. A. Nixon*

Centre right:
The last station south of Sheffield on the Midland main line still in the West Riding was the junction station of Dore & Totley, where the line west to Manchester diverged from the main line south to Derby. On 11 June 1963 'B1' class 4-6-0 No 61334 was pictured heading a Sheffield Midland-Manchester service through the station. *Ian Slater*

Below right:
The South Yorkshire Joint line was constructed during the early years of the 20th century to serve, primarily, a number of collieries in the area between Sheffield and Doncaster. Although passenger services were operated, these were never successful and were withdrawn finally in 1929 after a year's suspension three years earlier. The line, however, remained open and on 12 October 1963 'O4' No 63585 was photographed near Tickhill with an excursion organised by the Gainsborough Model Railway Society. Although relatively late, the South Yorkshire Joint served a number of important collieries, such as Dinnington, Markham Main and Maltby. As a result the route survived through the 1980s; its future must be considered uncertain, however, as a result of the recent closure of many of the Doncaster collieries.
A. Moyes

Mexborough (36B)
Allocation as at 1959

Class B1	61112, 61165, 61166, 61167, 61194
Class K3	61836, 61839, 61850, 61867, 61868
Class O4	63586, 63593, 63611, 63628, 63666, 63672, 63673, 63684, 63701, 63723, 63730, 63753, 63756, 63757, 63764, 63774, 63779, 63791, 63798, 63812, 63813, 63828, 63832, 63841, 63843, 63891, 63894, 63897, 63898, 63908
Class J11	64377, 64393, 64402, 64406
Class J69	68497, 68623
Class N5	69308
Class WD	90119, 90136, 90139, 90153, 90190, 90195, 90203, 90209, 90211, 90220, 90250, 90252, 90270, 90286, 90290, 90301, 90304, 90311, 90330, 90358, 90384, 90400, 90401, 90410, 90421, 90491, 90495, 90499, 90506, 90521, 90526, 90567, 90580, 90582, 90587, 90590, 90608, 90612, 90668, 90700

Left:
Underneath the wires at Sheffield Victoria 'J39/1' No 64744 undertakes station pilot duty on 7 June 1956. *Neil Caplan*

Left:
The Midland's station in Rotherham was Masborough and, until the opening of the replacement Rotherham Central station in 1986, acted as the town's only station for a number of years. 'Black 5' No 45428 stopped in the station *en route* from Holbeck to Tyseley light engine. The locomotive is now preserved on the North Yorkshire Moors Railway. *A. McBurnie*

Right:
Class B17 'Sandringham' No 61660 *Hull City*, allocated to 31B (March), is seen at Sheffield Victoria on 28 July 1950 with a Liverpool (Central)-Parkeston Quay express. Notice that Victoria has not yet received the catenary for the 1,500V dc electrification scheme that was to change the operation of the ex-Great Central route so radically. *Ian Allan Library*

Below:
D11 4-4-0 No 62663 *Prince Albert* waits outside Sheffield Victoria Station for a vacant platform, the Director is working the 12:30pm SO Chesterfield-Sheffield Victoria. On the left is a 350 HP 0-6-0 Diesel shunter in Blast Lane goods yard in September 1958. *K. R. Pirt.*

Eric Treacy's West Riding

Above:
No collection of photographs recalling steam operation in the West Riding would be complete without a selection of photographs by the late Eric Treacy. Many of his most evocative photographs were taken whilst he was at Halifax before returning to the West Riding as Bishop of Wakefield. His love of steam was legendary and perhaps he more than anyone was capable of evoking the memory of the great days of steam. First we see a line up of classic Eastern Region motive power at Leeds Central — 'N1' 0-6-2T No 69483, 'J50' No 68978 and 'A3' No 60055 *Woolwinder* — appropriately named for a photograph taken in one of the centres of the textile industry — about to depart on the up 'White Rose' express to King's Cross. *Eric Treacy*

Left:
Just south of Leeds on the ex-Great Northern main line to Doncaster was Beeston Junction, where the ex-GNR freight line to Parkside Junction — thus allowing freight trains to bypass central Leeds — diverged. This route closed on 3 July 1967 and today the scene would be radically different; the formation of the branch has been reclaimed and electrification masts run along the main line. Here we see 'J50' No 68900 coming off the branch from Parkside Junction with a mixed freight heading towards Wakefield.
Eric Treacy

Right:
Bradford (37C) allocated 'N1' No 69449 heads west towards Bradford Exchange with a Leeds Central-Bradford service at Holbeck. *Eric Treacy*

Below:
The crews of two 'Austerity' 2-8-0s keep a watchful eye as the locomotives — Nos 90321 (on the left) and 90385 — pass at Oakenshaw on coal trains on the Wakefield-Pontefract line. Both locomotives were allocated to Wakefield (56A) and so they were presumably quite used to meeting! No 90385 was withdrawn from Wakefield in March 1967, whilst No 90321 was transferred to Sunderland in December 1966 from where it was withdrawn in July 1967.
Eric Treacy

West Riding Preservation

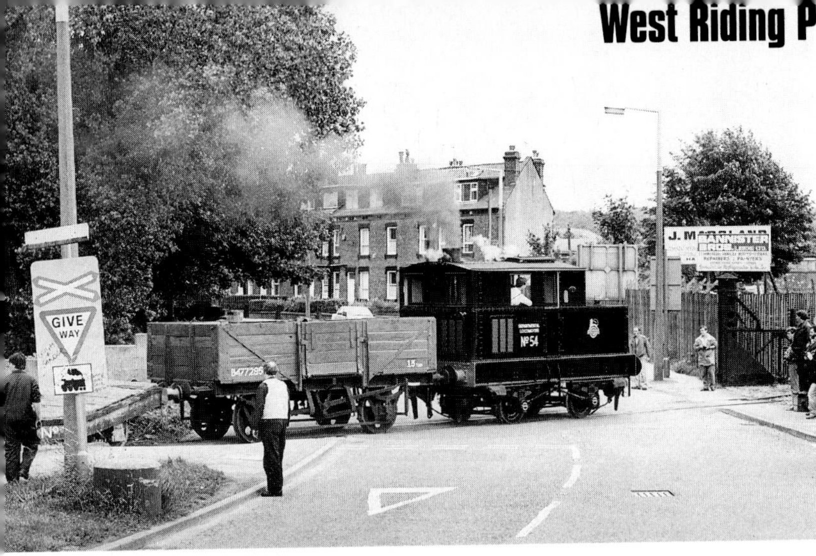

Left:
The first standard gauge preserved railway in Britain was the historic Middleton Railway. Here restored 'Y4' 0-4-0T No 54 crosses the road at Middleton with a demonstration freight on 17 July 1988. *Brian Dobbs*

Left:
The Keighley & Worth Valley took over the former Midland Railway branch on closure and has operated steam services for a quarter of a century. BR Class 4 4-6-0 No 75078 and USA TC 'S160' No 5820 double-head a six coach train up the gradient towards Oakworth on 4 April 1981.
John Sagar

Left:
A second section of the old Midland Railway to survive now forms the Yorkshire Dales Railway at Embsay. Haydock Foundry-built 0-4-0WT *Bellerophon* heads away from Embsay station with a service to Holywell on 17 July 1988.
Brian Dobbs